Macroeconomics in Focus

Macroeconomics in Focus

Martin Binks
Lecturer in Economics
University of Nottingham

and

Andrew Jennings
Lecturer in Economics
University of Nottingham

McGRAW-HILL Book Company (UK) Limited

London · New York · St Louis · San Francisco · Auckland · Bogotá · Guatemala
Hamburg · Johannesburg · Lisbon · Madrid · Mexico · Montreal · New Delhi
Panama · Paris · San Juan · São Paulo · Singapore · Sydney · Tokyo · Toronto

Published by
McGRAW-HILL Book Company (UK) Limited
MAIDENHEAD · BERKSHIRE · ENGLAND

British Library Cataloguing in Publication Data

Binks, Martin
Macroeconomics in focus
1. Macroeconomics
I. Title II. Jennings, Andrew
339 HB172.5

ISBN 0-07-084888-2

Library of Congress Cataloging-in-Publication Data

Binks, Martin.
Macroeconomics in focus.
Incudes bibliographies and index.
1. Macroeconomics. I. Jennings, Andrew. II. Title.
HB 172.5.B5 1986 339 85-24167
ISBN 0-07-084888-2

12345 CUP 89876

Typeset by Eta Services (Typesetters) Limited, Beccles, Suffolk,
and printed and bound in Great Britain at the University Press, Cambridge

To Alison and Lynne

Contents

Preface

This book provides an overview of modern macroeconomics. It presents a concise explanation of Keynesian economic intervention alongside the contrasting and more recent developments of the Monetarist and New Classical schools of thought.

For A level and undergraduate students of economics it is designed to complement the more detailed accounts of macroeconomics in modern textbooks by encompassing the subject in a very direct manner. By progressing swiftly through the main and often contentious issues, the book gives an overall perspective which is often necessarily prohibited in a purely textbook-orientated approach.

Apart from the particular needs of mainstream economics students, the authors have also attempted to cater for those who require or desire a better understanding of the macroeconomic debate but who do not need the exhaustive coverage which standard texts are designed to supply. This refers, for example, to students on courses which include a limited content of economics, people who feel that their occupation warrants a better understanding of the issues involved and those whose level of interest requires a more rigorous analysis than that available from the media.

In order to give an accurate explanation of the central areas under debate it is necessary to refer to quite complex analysis at some points. A more superficial treatment might be less challenging to the reader but it would also convey a false impression of the points at issue, many of which are by nature quite subtle. The book gives access to a rapid appraisal of the more relevant arguments in macroeconomics and also incorporates the technical detail needed by more specialist readers.

While aiming to contribute to a better understanding of macroeconomic theory the text also emphasizes the practical problems of government intervention in the economy. It is in order to highlight these problems that the book is published in conjunction with a computer-based macroeconomic simulation game for the BBC computer called 'Chancellor'.

This software enables the user to confront many of the decision-making exercises which Chancellors of the Exchequer face. It is designed to familiarize the user with some of the major relationships which can obtain between economic variables such as inflation, unemployment, investment and economic activity. It allows players to experience the uncertainty and imprecision which characterizes any attempt to 'steer' or 'control' an economy.

Both the book and game can be used independently. Their combination provides a unique insight to macroeconomics because it involves learning through both reading and actual experience.

An indication of the coverage of the text is available from the table of contents; a description of the main features of the 'Chancellor' game is included as the final chapter of the book. A short selection of additional reading is given at the end of each chapter.

We wish to acknowledge the typing assistance given by Lena Cavanagh and helpful observations made by referees; we take full responsibility for any remaining errors or shortcomings.

Martin Binks
Andrew Jennings
University of Nottingham

1.

Introduction to the macroeconomy

The study of economics is only necessary because of scarcity. There are insufficient goods and services to satisfy the demand for them by individuals, families and firms. People's labour, the land and machinery can only be combined to produce a certain quantity. The macroeconomy is the overall combination of these factors of production and the amount of goods and services which are produced in a given period of time. It describes in aggregate terms the allocations of the productive resources in an economy, and the distribution of the goods and services which result, to the people who live in it.

Systems of allocation

The system within which a macroeconomy operates depends upon the attitudes of the government in power. It also depends upon those measures taken by previous governments, since the effects of legislation and policy extend beyond the electoral term of those in office. There are two extremes of system between which most present-day economies lie, containing different proportions of the characteristics of each. One of these extremes can be described as a *pure market* economy, the other a *command* economy.

THE PURE MARKET SYSTEM

In its simplest form the pure market process allocates resources to production and the products to individuals through the price mechanism. While the most familiar markets to individuals are those for the goods and services which they consume, markets also exist in order to allocate any scarce resource which is involved in such production. Wages and salaries, rent, profit from the use of plant and machinery, and interest on loans are all prices in their respective markets. In a pure market system these prices would respond freely according to changes in the pattern of demand and supply in each particular market; they signal changes in relative scarcity and serve to adjust the pattern of usage of factors of production and the quantities of each good and service produced. If the market process were to work perfectly then the employment of the various factors of production would continually adapt to changes in demand so as to produce a unique pattern of goods and services; in theory the sum total of satisfaction or welfare would be maximized. A change in the demand for any particular good or service would be signalled through the price mechanism. This would refer not only to the market for the good or service concerned but also to the relevant factor markets dealing in the kind of labour, machinery, buildings, land and loans involved in its production. As the demand for these changed, all other things being equal, so would prices; a change in the allocation of the factors of production would ensue so that this new pattern of demand for final products would be met exactly at a new set of relative prices. Since the price mechanism permeates every aspect of economic activity under this system, its signalling ability is comprehensive in terms of changes in the conditions of both demand and supply. This communication system is based upon the operation of competition. As people compete to promote their own individual welfare they unconsciously promote the general welfare of society. This market process was described by Adam Smith, one of the earliest so-called 'Classical' economists, as the 'Invisible Hand'. The pure market system was judged by some economists in the nineteenth century to be so superior to any that people could devise and organize themselves that they encouraged policies to promote the forces of competition.

The problems of operating such a policy are many. The main ones stem from imperfections in the market mechanism along with its inability to satisfy certain 'moral' criteria which most people adopt.

Market imperfections

The operation of the price mechanism is not instantaneous: it takes time. Different markets are characterized by different time lags. The price of fresh vegetables on a market stall may change quite rapidly in response to changes in demand and supply. Moving labour from one production technique to another is more time consuming and costly, particularly if some retraining is involved. Economic prediction is uncertain. For the market system to work perfectly it would require that all consumers and producers have equal and free access to all information, a condition that can only be cited in theory.

Aside from time lags and imperfect information there are also many other barriers to the free movement of factors of production between different industries; restrictive practices and monopoly power are two examples out of many which perpetuate such market imperfections and corrupt the market process.

Apart from market imperfections which hinder the working of the price mechanism there is also the problem of the 'morality' of its effect. By allocating goods and services and factors of production through a price mechanism, each will receive more income as its contribution to the production process increases. With respect to labour, those who contribute more will command a higher price or wage which they can use to purchase goods and services. The very young, the aged, the severely disabled and others who are unable to make a significant contribution will likewise only command an insignificant amount of goods and services. This situation is deemed unacceptable in most economies, thus providing another reason for resistance to the free operation of market forces.

Perhaps more significantly, many economists believe that a system which attempted to allocate goods and services according to a measure of relative contribution and included a natural process of inherited ownership would perpetuate and create large inequalities in the distribution of wealth. Such disparities are potential sources of social tension and conflict.

A third problem which results from reliance upon a price mechanism concerns what economists refer to as 'externalities'. These are essentially either costs of production or consumption which are only partially borne by the producer or consumer. The market mechanism is largely unable to attribute such costs in a quantifiable way and so they are not completely incorporated in the producers' or consumers' calculations if they are included at all. The pollution of the environment due to industrial production and its consumption is just one example of a negative externality. Positive externalities may also occur, e.g., the construction of roads to service industry also benefits others as it improves the road system in general.

In an attempt to avoid these problems a much higher degree of control over the allocation of both factors of production and the material wealth which they produce may rest with government rather than market forces.

THE COMMAND ECONOMY

Under the opposite extreme, the factors of production and the goods and services which they produce are allocated by government decree rather than market forces. This, in theory, avoids the problems which can occur when relying solely on the market mechanism, because the government can simply choose to avoid them. The major problem which arises under this system, however, is how to ensure that the factors of production and associated products are distributed in the 'best' way in the absence of market signals. How can government decide the way in which factors of production should be employed to produce the pattern of goods and services most suited to the needs and desires of the population? If, as they are almost bound to do, they make errors of judgement, then there will tend to be shortages of some goods and services and surpluses of others. The productive resources of the economy will be misallocated and therefore combined inefficiently. There is wastage of productive potential. A further possible weakness of the pure command system is that those who decide the allocation processes are open to corruption and the abuse of considerable powers. This is analogous to the case of monopoly power in market economies. There are many further points which could be made on the strengths and weaknesses of the pure command system, but these are not central to the purpose of this book.

The historical debate

As a result of the many problems faced by each of these extreme systems of allocation, all economies contain a mixture of the two. The extent to which they favour one system over the other depends upon the political and economic views of past and present governments. It is important to remember that all economies vary both through time and one from another. In a sense therefore there can never be a definitive explanation of macroeconomics which is entirely appropriate or up to date: there is always scope for debate.

By the late 1930s the arguments over how best to manage the macroeconomy had fallen into two distinct schools of thought, the Classical or free market school and the Keynesian. While the Keynesian view predominated throughout the 1950s and 1960s, there was an apparent failure of this thinking to address the economic problems of the 1970s. This resulted in a re-emergence of the Classical school's view in the form of two alternatives, Modern Monetarism and the

New Classical school; this in turn led the Keynesians to reappraise their own position.

The main points at issue are the extent and nature of government intervention required to achieve a particular set of economic objectives.

In broad terms, most governments consider five main economic indicators as a measure of their contribution to economic progress, though most would agree that their simultaneous achievement in practice is almost impossible. These aims can be stated as follows:

1. A 'satisfactory' rate of economic growth (3 per cent or more)
2. A 'low' level of unemployed factors of production (3 per cent or less)
3. Stable prices or only a 'moderate' rate of price inflation (3 per cent or less)
4. An approximate balance between imports and exports in terms of their value
5. A 'stable' currency (fluctuating by no more than 5 per cent in value in any year, as measured in terms of other currencies)

(The definitions of the above terms will vary in practice, but approximate rates and levels are given in brackets as examples.)

Prior to the 1930s most economists believed that these objectives could be best achieved through the operation of the price mechanism. This Classical view of the operation of the economy in its totality was based upon an 'idealized' model of the market system. The implicit theory of macroeconomics which this provides can be derived from Say's law. This is based upon the writings of J. B. Say, a French economist and follower of Adam Smith. This law can be stated simply as 'supply creates its own demand'. The price mechanism adjusts until the demand is equal to the quantity supplied.

When applied to the labour market the clear implication of this view is that involuntary unemployment is not possible in the long term. There may be short-term conditions in which factors of production lie idle, but these will be removed through the price mechanism; their price will fall until they can be gainfully employed. There is therefore a natural tendency for the economy to operate at, or move towards, a condition of 'full employment'; it is self-equilibrating. For this process to work efficiently, however, it was considered vital that market forces should operate as freely as possible. Government intervention might only serve to distort the market process and so governments were urged, as far as was practical and morally acceptable, to leave the economy alone, except where policies were required to facilitate the efficient operation of the market.

The protracted economic depression of the 1920s and 1930s undermined this conventional view that full employment was the natural state of affairs; it was no longer clear that divergences from that state would be self-correcting through the responses of the market. The conventional wisdom was under threat and alternative explanations were put forward. These referred primarily to the role of government in the market and the ways by which it could intervene in the economy in order to better achieve the main aims set out above. A prime mover in this debate about the role and nature of government intervention in the economy was John Maynard Keynes.

In his book '*The General Theory of Employment, Interest, And Money*', published in 1936, usually referred to simply as 'The General Theory', Keynes sought to demonstrate that capitalist market economies would not necessarily or naturally move towards an equilibrium level of economic activity which corresponds to 'full employment'. The Classical economic view that there was an automatic tendency for it to do so via the price mechanism was, he considered, inappropriate. The high levels of unemployment during the 'Great Depression' appeared to call for an alternative explanation of the main economic interrelationships involved. Keynes concentrated on the dynamic characteristics of an economy's behaviour. No economy is ever still in the sense that the same factors of production are employed in the same way to produce the same pattern of goods and services for the same population. Economies are ever changing. Keynes was concerned with the economics of disequilibrium. He was concerned with the ways by which government could affect the direction which an economy takes, rather than the measures required to achieve a particular equilibrium condition. The essence of his message was that the level of economic activity in an economy was primarily determined by the demand for such activity, the demand for the goods and services which it produces.

Keynes' theories did not, in themselves, provide a determinate explanation of how economies behave, because they were based upon the notion of disequilibrium rather than equilibrium. As a result his theories have been subjected to various reinterpretations. The nature and characteristics of an economy are fluid rather than static, so the application of 'Keynesian' principles should always involve a reinterpretation of Keynesian doctrine in order to adapt or apply it to the prevailing conditions. The underlying principle, however, is that the demand for goods and services inspires their supply.

One of the most well known interpretations of Keynes' system was provided by Professors J. R. Hicks and A. H. Hansen. Ironically, in the light of the above, its popularity stemmed from the fact that it reduces the dynamic Keynesian system to a set of equilibrium conditions. By doing so it makes possible the kind of analysis which was, and is, most popular in economics; the comparison of one equilibrium position with another. Instead of considering the ways by which the direction that an economy takes can be influenced through the government's own spending activities, both Hicks and Hansen concentrated on the different equilibrium conditions which would follow from a specific change in such policies, *ceteris paribus*, 'all other things remaining the same'. The model which was presented as a formal interpretation of the 'General Theory' is known as the *IS–LM* model. *IS* refers to the equilibrium of investment and savings while *LM* refers to the equality of the demand and the supply of money.

In summary, Keynes' major departure from the Classical model of the economy was in his rejection of Say's law that supply created its own demand. Keynes focused upon the *demand* for, rather than the supply of, goods and services as the prime determinant of the level of economic activity. He did not believe that the price mechanism adjusted with sufficient speed to guarantee that all supply would be cleared in the market; in the case of labour there could be persistent involuntary unemployment. Since previously the fortunes of the macroeconomy had been trusted largely to the operation of the market, Keynes' alternative interpretation represented a radically different explicit model of macroeconomic relationships, the effects of which still influence political economic thinking.

By the late 1970s a new problem of accelerating inflation associated with prolonged and persistent unemployment had arisen to confront policy makers and economists. It appeared that the traditional application of Keynesian policies had failed. Keynesian economists returned to Keynes' original writings in search of new and relevant interpretations while others referred to the teachings of the Classical school for an explanation and policy prescription. Two distinct schools of thought have arisen from the resurgence of Classical economics, namely the Modern Monetarists and the New Classical economists. Both have questioned the very core of Keynesian economics, casting doubt on the ability and wisdom of governments in their attempts to bring about beneficial economic change.

The four chapters that follow develop a formal model of the Keynesian *IS–LM* framework. Chapter 6 presents the Monetarist and New Classical alternatives, highlighting the major points of disagreement between these and the Keynesians. Chapters 7 and 8 discuss the policy prescriptions proposed by each and the practical problems of implementing them.

The Chancellor game

The 'Chancellor' game referred to in the preface is largely founded upon Keynesian principles, but the actual form of the relationships draws upon more recent interpretations of macroeconomics, along with some recognition of modern macroeconomic events such as stagflation. The user should gain an understanding of the demand-based interpretation of macroeconomics, along with an appreciation of the need for a continual reappraisal of the theory in the light of changes in the way economies behave. The reader should never lose sight of the fact that Keynes was concerned with a continually changing economy rather than the comparative static approach which has had to be used in 'Chancellor'. Users of the game should recognize, however, that many actions of intervention involve a time lag in their effect, as do many of the interrelationships between the economic variables involved. The economy will still change even if the Chancellor does nothing.

In order not to distract attention from the analysis which follows, further consideration of the 'Chancellor' game is postponed until the final two chapters of the book.

Additional reading

1. Barber, W. J. (1967) *A History of Economic Thought*, Penguin.
2. Bator, F. M. 'The Anatomy of Market Failure', *Quarterly Journal of Economics*, 1958.
3. Hahn, F. 'Reflections on the Invisible Hand', *Lloyds Bank Review*, April, 1982.
4. Klamer, A. (1984) *The New Classical Macroeconomics*, Wheatsheaf. (Mainly Chapter 1.)
5. Leijonhufvud, A. (1968) *On Keynesian Economics and the Economics of Keynes*, Oxford University Press.
6. Smith, A. (1970) *The Wealth of Nations*, Penguin.

2.

Aggregate demand

The application of Keynesian policies in most Western mixed economies introduced a form of government intervention which still persists despite changing views of its desirability. In order to understand modern macroeconomics it is important to consider in detail the nature of aggregate demand since it underlies so much of Keynesian theory and policy. In the Keynesian sense, aggregate demand is the most important element of the macroeconomy.

In order to develop the Keynesian interpretation it is useful to consider the macroeconomy as a flow of economic activity. Consider a simple economy containing only households and firms. Households provide firms with factors of production for which they receive incomes as payment. Firms employ the factors to produce goods and services which are sold to the households. This can be illustrated as in Figure 2.1.

The level of national income in one year is determined by the speed of this flow; the faster it is, the more goods and services are produced and the higher is national income. According to the Keynesians the speed of this flow is itself determined by the amount of demand for the goods and services which results; this is known as the level of aggregate demand.

All incomes received within the flow can be spent on the consumption of goods and services or saved. Expenditure on consumption represents the demand for those goods and services bought; savings or deferred consumption represents a leakage or withdrawal of potential demand from the flow. The goods and services produced in the flow can be divided into two categories, those for immediate consumption and those for investment. Investment refers to the accumulation of stocks and the creation of the means of production: plant and machinery. Investment constitutes an additional injection of demand for goods and services into the circular flow. The concept of injections and withdrawals of demand into and from the flow is important because

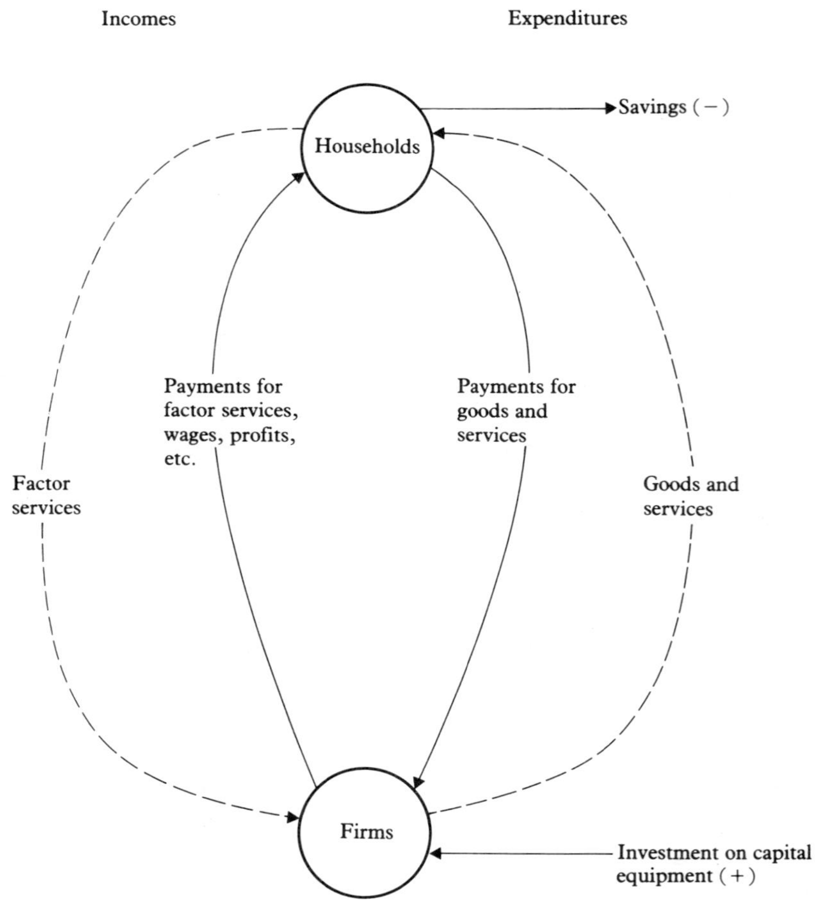

Figure 2.1 *The circular flow of incomes and expenditures*

the balance between the two affects the speed or level of activity. If more potential demand is leaking from the flow in savings than is being injected as investment then the flow slows down; national income is falling. National income rises while injections exceed withdrawals. When the two are equal the economy is in equilibrium. This is a hypothetical situation which is used in theoretical analysis to refer to a constant level of economic activity; national income is unchanging. In equilibrium planned and realized saving are exactly equal to planned and realized investment. Although the decisions to save and invest are made independently by different groups of people, a change in either planned saving or planned investment will affect the speed of the flow and the realized levels of each. One theme in much of the analysis which follows concerns how, *in theory*, realized saving and investment are equated to provide an equilibrium level of income.

Keynesians believe that the macroeconomy is dynamic: it is always changing and is therefore in a perpetual state of disequilibrium. Macroeconomic policy represents an attempt to steer an economy along a particular course rather than to achieve a specific set of objectives in perpetuity. The course is usually defined in terms of specific economic variables as referred to briefly above, i.e. economic growth, employment, prices, balance of payments and the currency. From a Keynesian viewpoint these variables are influenced in various ways by the level and rate of change of aggregate demand. By varying its own contribution to aggregate demand, government is able to affect the policy variables and to some extent determine the course which they take. This process of government intervention is highly imperfect. Government can at best expect to receive only a vague picture of where the economy has been, because measuring variables like employment, unemployment, inflation, the balance of trade and the level of economic activity is so difficult and involves so many errors. Their attempt to control it is based upon their interpretation of that picture. In order to explain how the macroeconomy may have behaved in the past, it is necessary to construct a highly oversimplified model of it to highlight the role of the main forces at work and the ways in which they affect each other. If it were assumed that these underlying relationships would persist in the future, it is possible to gain an indication of how governments should intervene to influence economic progress. It is this *aggregate demand management* which is considered in the chapters which follow.

Aggregate demand consists of several different elements, each of which needs separate consideration, because they differ in terms of the main variables which influence them. Four separate elements will be considered below; these are:

1. Consumption demand
2. Investment demand
3. Government demand
4. Trade

The sum of these can be regarded as the level of *gross national product* (GNP).

This accounting identity can be formalized as:

$$Y = C + I + G + (X - M)$$

Where

$Y = GNP$
C = consumption expenditure
I = investment expenditure
G = government expenditure
X = export income
M = import expenditure
thus $(X - M)$ = the balance of trade

It should be stressed that all these variables, unless stated otherwise, are incorporated in the analysis in what economists call 'real' terms. This means that their value is measured in terms of the goods and services that they represent, irrespective of changes in prices. Prices determine the final 'nominal' value of goods and services.

Consumption demand

This refers to the total demand for goods and services for consumption by individuals, households and firms over a specified time period. When constructing hypotheses of the main determinants of the level of consumption, economists have usually considered the case of a single individual and then generalized it to the population as a whole. While individuals will vary in their reaction to them, the main influences upon consumption decisions which are considered here are as follows:

(*a*) Income
(*b*) Rate of interest
(*c*) Expectations
(*d*) Stocks of financial assets or durable consumer goods
(*e*) Age distribution of population

INCOME

In Keynes' interpretation, current disposable income is by far the most significant determinant of the level of consumption expenditure in the short run. Taking the case of the individual as a starting point he related higher income to higher levels of consumption. He did not assume that this would bear a simple proportionate relationship where with no income the individual would spend nothing, and as income rose a fixed proportion of it would be allocated to consumption. To summarize his view, it is helpful to consider the relationship between income and consumption in terms of the average and marginal propensities to consume.

The average propensity to consume (*APC*) over any given time period is simply the ratio of consumption expenditure to disposable income:

$$APC = C/Y^d$$

where C = expenditure on goods and services for consumption and Y^d = disposable income. If all income is spent on consumption then the $APC = 1$.

The marginal propensity to consume (*MPC*) is the proportion of any change in income which is allocated to consumption.

$$MPC = dC/dY^d$$

where d refers to the change in each. If the *MPC* were 0.5 then, given a rise in disposable income of £1, the rise in planned consumption of goods and services would be 50 pence.

Keynes assumed that with no income an individual will either borrow or spend some of his savings, i.e., dissave, in order to continue consumption expenditures. In a sense, therefore, the *APC* in this situation is infinite because a positive expenditure on consumption is divided by zero income. Keynes himself felt that as income rises the proportion of any rise which an individual spends on consumption will tend to be lower the higher the level of income. In relative terms a rich person would spend less of a £1 increase in income on consumpton than a poor person would; the *MPC* declines as income rises.

Given this *consumption function* both the average and marginal propensities to consume decline as income rises. This theory of the relationship between disposable income and consumption is called the *absolute income hypothesis* because the level of consumption is determined by the absolute level of current disposable income.

Following Keynes' hypothesis a great deal of empirical work was undertaken which sought to test the absolute income model against the then newly available national income data. Foremost in this area was a study by the American Simon Kuznets, published in 1946. The conclusions of his study were twofold. First, the absolute income theory of the consumption function could be justifiably simplified by assuming that the *MPC* is constant, and, second, there was a distinction between consumption behaviour in the short and long runs.

The assumption of a constant *MPC* leads to the consumption function shown in Figure 2.2. If the level of consumption at zero disposable

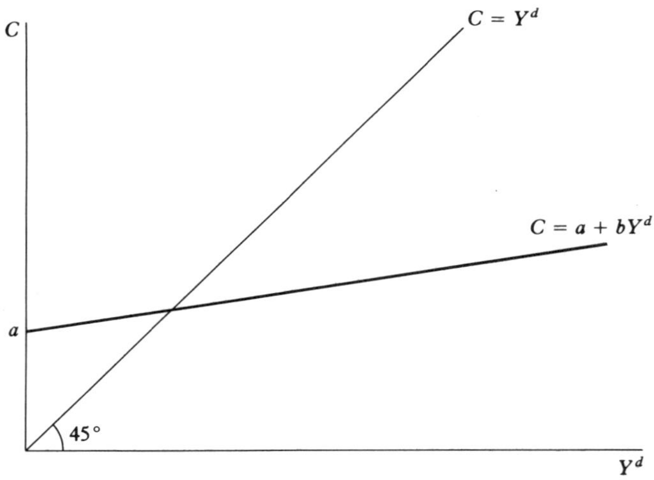

Figure 2.2 *The absolute income hypothesis*

income is a and the slope of the function, the *MPC*, is b then it can be represented algebraically as

$$C = a + bY^d$$

Consumption expenditure at any given level of disposable income is the sum of the autonomous element, a and the *MPC*, b, multiplied by that level of disposable income.

One of the most important properties of this function is that at all levels of income $MPC < APC$. This implies that if disposable income falls people will protect their living standards by not cutting consumption expenditure proportionally, and that, conversely, as disposable income rises consumption will not rise proportionally. The acceptance of these ideas led, in the 1940s, to the formulation of the *stagnation thesis*. This implied that as national income grew the relative contribution of consumption would fall because the *APC* was falling.

Recalling that national income may be expressed as

$$Y = C + I + G + (X - M)$$

and assuming that the relative importance of I and $(X - M)$, i.e., I/Y and $(X - M)/Y$, are unlikely to change, it follows that income growth will stagnate unless government expenditures are increased, that is, G/Y rises as income rises so as to counteract the relative decline in consumption. It was for this reason that Keynes saw a central role for both the consumption function and government in his model of the macroeconomy. This was in stark contrast to the earlier view adopted by the Classical school.

The distinction in the relationship over different periods of time stems from considering two different types of data. Short-run models were examined by using both cross-section and time-series consumption and income data. Cross-section data refer to recorded observations on individuals or families in different income groups, together with their respective consumption expenditures at a specific point in time. This approach is akin to a snapshot of consumption expenditure across different income groups. The time-series data refer to aggregate values of income and consumption over a number of years. In this particular context, a series of between 10 and 15 years' data would be considered. The long-run studies were based entirely on time-series data of a 40–50 year time-span.

The short-run data supported a function as shown in Figure 2.2, with a positive value for *a*. However, Kuznets concluded that longer data sets indicated a proportional relationship between income and consumption expenditures. This implies a function which passes directly through the origin; the *APC* is constant. These two findings are set out in Figure 2.3.

The long-run function in Figure 2.3 is given by the line $C = bY$. It was proposed that the cyclical variations in national income caused the short-run relationship to shift through time. In doing so, it 'maps

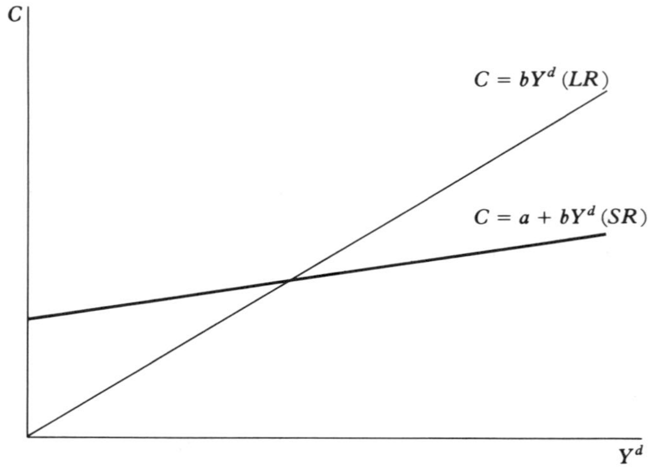

Figure 2.3 *Short- and long-run consumption functions*

out' the underlying relationship between consumption and income. In the light of the above comments and the stagnation thesis, it is important to note that in this underlying relationship $MPC = APC$ and there is no long-term tendency for the relative importance of consumption expenditure to decline.

Publication of these findings led to a number of alternative formulations of the consumption function, the three most important of which are considered below.

The relative income hypothesis

This was presented in a revised version by James Duesenberry in a book published in 1949. In it he refers to the 'emulative' and 'imitative' characteristics of consumption activity; he also began by considering the behaviour of a single individual. He believed that in the long run people based their consumption expenditure on that of the people with whom they tended to associate. The proportion of income spent on consumption would therefore depend on the size of their income relative to those of their social group. If their income was relatively low in this context they would tend to spend a relatively high proportion of it in order to 'keep up' and vice versa. Some rather contentious evidence which was cited in support of this hypothesis referred to the *APC* of black and white families in one part of the USA who earned about $5000 per annum. This showed that the white families spent a higher proportion of their income on consumption than did the black families. The reason for this, it was claimed, was that in 'white society' \$5000 was relatively lower as a level of income than it was in 'black society' and therefore the white families had to spend a higher proportion of it in order to be able to emulate and imitate the consumption behaviour of their associates. The point is clear despite the nature of the evidence.

In the short run, people would tend to use their past peak income as a benchmark to determine their level of consumption expenditure. Thus, if income fell, they would spend a higher proportion of the new level of income on consumption in an attempt to preserve their relative standard of living. This behavioural pattern is consistent with the Keynesian notion of $MPC < APC$ and also with the findings of Kuznets.

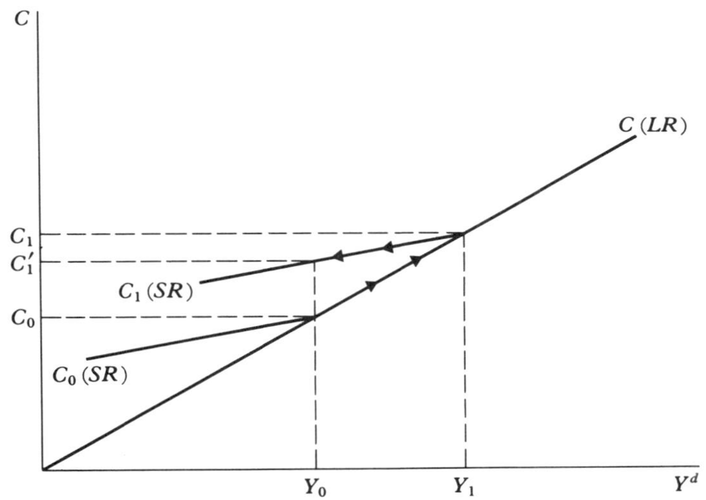

Figure 2.4 *The relative income hypothesis*

If the distribution of income remains unchanged, then according to this hypothesis so will the proportion of it which is devoted to consumption, even if the overall level changes: relative incomes are constant. This in turn implies that as income grows past the previous peak level a relationship where $MPC = APC$ should be observed.

In Figure 2.4, if income grew from Y_0 to Y_1, consumption would expand along the line $C(LR)$, $MPC = APC$. However, if income were to fall back from the peak level of Y_1, consumers would attempt to maintain their standard of living and consumption would decline along $C(SR)$, $MPC < APC$: consumption expenditures are cut less than proportionally to income. This effect is referred to as the 'ratchet effect' and helps to accommodate the apparent contradiction arising from the empirical evidence.

The permanent and life-cycle hypotheses

Two further theories of consumption behaviour relevant to modern macroeconomics are the *permanent income hypothesis* proposd by Milton Friedman in 1957 and the *life-cycle hypothesis* developed by A. Ando and F. Modigliani in the early 1960s. The similarities between these two theories outweigh their differences and so it is convenient to discuss them together.

Although the objective of the theories was the same as that of Duesenberry, namely, to reconcile the empirical evidence, they both made two important theoretical developments. First, emphasis was changed from consumption expenditure to consumption itself, and second, the main determinant of this consumption was seen to be wealth, not current disposable income.

Consumption expenditure refers to the actual amount of income spent on consumption goods. The majority of goods that are bought are non-durable and the flow of benefits received from those goods is short-lived. Thus expenditure on a chocolate bar or newspaper is usually followed by immediate consumption. This is not so, however, in the case of durable commodities like cars and houses. Such commodities continue to yield consummable services long after their initial expenditure has been covered. The implication is that to consider an individual's or an economy's consumption simply in terms of expenditures on goods and services will be a misrepresentation of the actual level of consumption.

The permanent and life-cycle theories also recognized that it was possible for an individual to break the direct relationship between consumption and income by borrowing or lending. Consumption of certain commodities, particularly durables, may be brought forward by borrowing against future income. The constraint on the level of consumption an individual or economy can enjoy is therefore not current income but some measure of wealth based on all past, current and future incomes. Friedman called this concept *permanent income*, while

Ando and Modigliani refer to the *life-cycle* of income for an individual.

A typical individual with a life span of T years might be expected to spend more on consumption than he earns in income as a child and young adult. This excess of consumption over income being provided; usually from family. In his earning years he will tend to save 'for his old age' in the form of pension schemes, etc. In his retirement he will spend these savings and his consumption expenditure will exceed his earned income.

If the age distribution of the population is constant in the long run, Ando and Modigliani show that such consumption behaviour is consistent with a model where $MPC = APC$. Likewise for high current-income families in the middle years of life we would expect to observe a relatively low APC, because Y is greater than C, e.g., point t_0 in Figure 2.5, and at lower income levels in young and old age, points t_1

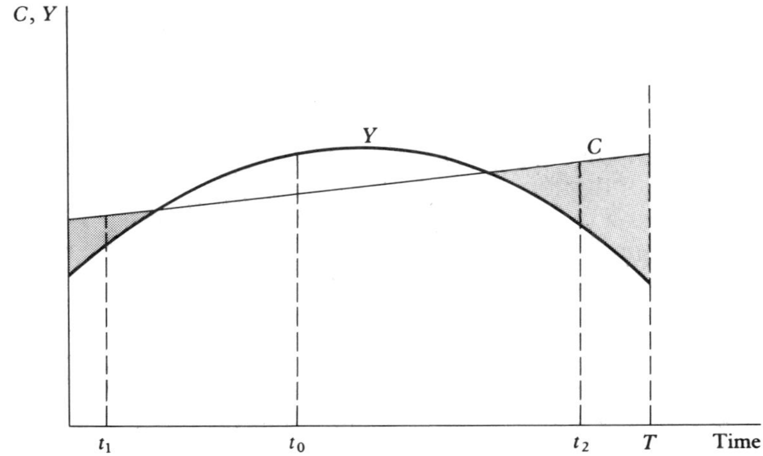

Figure 2.5 *The life-cycle hypothesis*

and t_2, C is greater than Y and hence a relatively high APC would be observed. The theory is thus consistent with the cross-section budget studies which reveal a declining APC as the level of *current income* rises.

Friedman is able to draw conclusions similar to those of the life-cycle hypothesis by drawing a distinction between permanent and transitory income and permanent and transitory consumption. Again taking the case of the individual, he claimed that people did not adjust their consumption behaviour as their income changed, but that they distinguished between permanent and transitory changes. Where a change in income was regarded as permanent, consumption expenditure would change in response as consumers attempt to smooth their actual income stream into a more or less flat consumption pattern. Where a change in income is regarded as transitory or temporary, the individual will not react by changing consumption expenditure. An example of a transitory change in income would be a temporary loss of overtime income due to illness, or an unexpected bonus of some kind, like a win on the horses. People treat such changes as deviations from the norm, which do not have a significant effect upon the individual's or family's wealth and thus they do not adjust their level of consumption. Even if a transitory gain was spent on a durable asset, the effect on consumption, as defined above, would be small. Similarly, an example of transitory consumption would be to set out with the intent to purchase a good, only to find that it is out of stock, or to see a product available in a 'sale' and purchase it, having not previously planned to do so. The transitory components of income and consumption can therefore be both negative and positive. Friedman believes that in the long run the transitory components of income will cancel out, as will those of consumption. Transitory income will not affect transitory consumption. In the long run there is a constant relationship between income and consumption because *permanent consumption* is a constant proportion of *permanent income.*

THE RATE OF INTEREST

If the rate of interest is regarded simply as the price of borrowed money, then a change in it might be expected to affect consumption in the opposite direction: there is an inverse relationship between the two. If the rate of interest rises, consumption expenditure financed with borrowed money is more expensive and that expenditure is therefore reduced. This effect would be reinforced due to the increased inducement to save. At face value the relationship appears simple and predictable. A complication is introduced, however, by the fact that many people save in order to fund a specific purchase in the future. The higher the rate of interest the less it is necessary to save in order to ensure a specific amount at some point in the future. The net effect of a change in the rate of interest is therefore more difficult to predict.

EXPECTATIONS

Expectations are a powerful economic variable influencing consumption expenditure though, again, the relationship is not clear cut. In the short run highly pessimistic expectations tend to raise consumption. If for example people expect to be involved directly or indirectly in war, they tend to stockpile some kinds of consumption goods like tinned food. In the medium or longer term the role of price expectations might be expected to affect people's spending habits. If the general level of prices is expected to rise, one reaction could be that people will tend to spend more on consumption in order to avoid paying the higher prices which are expected to prevail in the future. This might be reinforced by the disincentive to save, which such expectations would constitute. If the general level of prices rises, then the real value of money in terms of the goods and services which it can be used to purchase is reduced, unless the rate of interest rises sufficiently to offset the price effect. This relationship could be reversed, however, if people maintain their level of savings in real terms. In this case a rise in the price level would cause savings to rise and consumption to fall as people increase the money value of their savings in line with prices.

STOCKS OF FINANCIAL OR DURABLE ASSETS

The relationship which would be expected to obtain here is probably more straightforward than those described above. The larger the stocks of financial assets held by a society, the less motivated they are to accumulate further stocks and the more of their income they spend on consumption. The larger the stocks of durable consumer goods held, the fewer people need to buy, but the more services they need to maintain them.

AGE DISTRIBUTION

The main point here follows from the life-cycle hypothesis described above. In the long run the *APC* would be expected to change if the age structure of the population changes. If for example the proportion of middle-aged people rose, then the *APC* would be expected to fall as they tend to save more to cater for consumption expenditure in old age.

As is clear from the above, there is some disagreement as to the effect which the main influences have upon consumption. No consumption function will fully predict consumption because the relative roles of the many factors involved are always changing.

Investment demand

This refers to the total demand for goods and services for investment. At this point it is useful to distinguish between *net investment* and *gross investment*. Net investment refers to changes in the size of the stock of capital, while gross investment includes that which is required to replace capital no longer operable, e.g., plant and machinery which has worn out. Investment is probably most easily, if crudely, conceptualized as the demand for those goods and services needed for production. The resulting products may be designed for consumption or investment themselves. They may for example be used to manufacture products like food and clothing, or to provide services such as hairdressing for immediate consumption, or in turn to facilitate the production of further capital goods. Investment in this case refers to the demand for capital formation to employ in the production process; it should not be confused with investment in financial institutions like building societies or bank deposit accounts, for example, as these are not 'investments' but forms of saving. They may be used for capital formation eventually through the issuing of loans or equity funds, but the concern here is with the actual employment of capital in production. To oversimplify greatly, if production were seen to result from the interaction of men and machines, then investment in this context refers to the creation and use of machines.

The main influences upon the investment decision which are considered here are as follows:

(*a*) The rate of interest
(*b*) Expectations
(*c*) The rate of change of income
(*d*) The level of income
(*e*) Technological change

THE RATE OF INTEREST

People 'invest' or 'defer consumption' in order to receive a 'return' on their investment in the future. By purchasing a particular machine and employing it in the production process the investor anticipates making a profit over and above the cost of the machine and its running costs. This concept of a return on capital employed is vital for an understanding of the investment decision, and helps to explain the role in that decision of both the rate of interest and that of expectations. Concern here is restricted, initially, to the rate of interest.

Put simply, the rate of interest can be regarded as the 'price' of loan finance or conversely the return to the lender of providing it. As such it represents to the investor either the cost of borrowing funds to buy investment goods and services or, if he plans to use his own finance, the alternative return which he would expect to receive from lending that money to someone else. The decision to invest funds directly in capital formation, such as the purchase of a machine, implies that the investor expects to receive a higher return in this way than the rate of interest would provide from lending the money elsewhere. In order to calculate whether the investment project under consideration will yield a higher rate of return than the rate of interest it is necessary to consider why interest rates exist and how they are used in a technique called *discounting*. (The determination of interest rates will be considered further in Chapter 4.)

Interest rates exist primarily because of what economists term 'time preference'. This refers to the fact that people prefer money now rather than a guarantee of the same amount at some point in the future. As has been stated already, interest rates represent the price which must be paid in order to persuade the lender of funds to forgo the immediate consumption which they could otherwise afford. This describes the 'real' rate of interest. The 'nominal' or actual rate prevailing on a particular day may include some allowance for the rate of change of prices at that time. The 'real' rate of interest reflects the operation of 'time preference' while the actual rate allows for the fact that price inflation is eroding the 'real' value of money in terms of the amount of goods and services which a given amount can purchase. Put simply, if the 'nominal' rate of interest was 20 per cent and the rate of inflation was 10 per cent then, in theory, the 'real' rate of interest would be 10 per cent, i.e., the nominal rate minus the rate of inflation. It is important to make this distinction because in periods of sustained price rises people may tend to assume that interest rates exist simply to counteract inflation. Even if there was no price inflation, interest rates would still exist because of time preference.

The problem for the investor is therefore to compare the potential rewards for deferring consumption in order to finance an investment project with those which would arise from lending the money at the market rate of interest. The purchase of capital goods or services incurs an immediate cost while the incomes which they generate are received in the future. It is not sufficient that the simple arithmetical sum of these future incomes exceeds the total costs of the project. This is because sums of money received in the future are worth less than the same amount of money received in the present, even if there is no inflation. The reason for this lies with the rate of interest.

To illustrate this principle consider the offer of a gift of £100 either now or one year hence, with the current market rate of interest at 10 per cent. The £100 received now could be invested to take advantage of this rate of interest and would have grown to the sum of £110 in a year's time. This is clearly greater than the alternative offer of £100 a year hence, and therefore the 'present value' of £100 now is greater than £100 in a year's time. The present value of the £100 a year hence would be the sum, which if invested now at 10 per cent, would be worth £100 in a year's time. This sum must be less than £100.

Algebraically

$$V = S(1 + r)$$

where

V = value after one year
S = initial sum
r = market rate of interest

In the example, S = £100 and r = 10 per cent, thus

$$V = £100\,(1 + 0.1)$$
$$V = £110$$

It follows that the present value of the £110 in a year's time is £100

i.e., $$\frac{£110}{(1 + 0.1)} = £100$$

or more generally

$$PV = \frac{V}{(1 + r)}$$

Where PV = present value. This expression is the essence of the discounting technique, and shows the use of the rate of interest to 'reduce' a future sum to its present value.

The present value of the £100 received in a year's time would be

$$PV = \frac{£100}{(1 + 0.1)}$$
$$\simeq £91$$

and thus the discounting process reveals that the time-scale of the two gifts is vital in determining their relative worth. In the context of an investment project it is clear that a project having an initial outlay of £100 and a net income of £100 in a year's time would not be desirable even though the two figures superficially imply that no loss would be made.

The above reasoning can be extended to periods greater than one year. For example the value of £100 in two year's time at 10 per cent would be £121.

$$£121 = £100(1 + 0.1)(1 + 0.1)$$

and thus the present value of £121 is

$$PV = \frac{£121}{(1 + 0.1)(1 + 0.1)} = \frac{£121}{(1 + 0.1)^2} = £100$$

In general the present value of a sum V to be received n years ahead at a rate of interest r would be

$$PV = \frac{V}{(1 + r)^n}$$

and where sums are received at different points in time over a period of n years as

$$PV = V_0 + \frac{V_1}{(1 + r)} + \frac{V_2}{(1 + r)^2} + \cdots + \frac{Vn}{(1 + r)^n}$$

There are two ways by which the discounting technique can be used in order to explain the apparently prime role played by the rate of interest in the investment decision. The first of these involves the calculation of the *net present value* of the profits or returns of the project. The second requires the calculation of the *internal rate of return*. The meaning of each of these will be made clearer below.

The calculation of net present value

The calculation of the net present value (NPV) of the project requires estimates for three separate cost and revenue elements. These are: first, the initial purchase price of the capital involved; second, the anticipated running costs incurred in its employment; and third, the expected revenues which result from the sale of the product concerned. The first of these, the initial outlay involved, is often quite easy to ascertain from the suppliers of the capital goods and services concerned. The running costs and the revenues from the sales of the product are less easy to predict. Their prediction requires a variety of forecasts. Before considering some of the problems which arise in the making of these, it is useful to consider the calculation of net present value as if the requisite data were available, implying complete certainty about the future. This involves a process of cumulative discounting to reduce future returns to their present value. This calculation can be represented as follows:

$$NPV = R_0 + R_1/(1 + r) + R_2/(1 + r)^2 + \cdots + R_n/(1 + r)^n$$

where

NPV = net present value
R = the real return or net cash flow in the period having allowed for inflation
r = the real rate of interest
R_0 = includes the cost of the project and will therefore usually be a negative number.

To use a simple example – consider an investment project of three years' duration by the end of which the plant and machinery involved would be worthless. There is no return until the first full year of the project when, ignoring for the moment the cost of the machine, the potential investor expects to incur costs of £100 and to receive revenues from sales of £210. The net cash flow expected in the first full year of operation R_1 is therefore £110. In the second year a net cash flow of £121 is expected, while in the final year a figure of £133 is anticipated. If the rate of interest is 10 per cent, then this project has a present value of £300 because there is no return in R_0; in R_1 £110 is received which, when discounted by the rate of interest, is worth £100; in the second year £121 is divided by 1.21 (i.e., 1.1 × 1.1); and in the final year the rate of interest must be applied three times (i.e., 1.1 × 1.1 × 1.1) which means dividing the return for that year by 1.33. Thus

$$\begin{aligned} PV &= 0 + £100 + £100 + £100 \\ &= £300 \end{aligned}$$

where PV = present value.

One way of understanding this process more easily is to imagine it in reverse. If £100 is lent out at a rate of interest of 10 per cent, it would be worth £110 after one year, £121 after 2 years (i.e., £110 + 10 per cent of £110), and £133 after three years. Returning to the example, the present value of the investment is £300; if the cost of the initial capital formation R_0 is £290 then the project has a positive *net* present value of £10. This means that if the estimates of revenues and costs are correct, and the interest rate remains at 10 per cent, then the investor will make £10 more by investing in the project than would be received from lending the money elsewhere at a rate of interest of 10 per cent. Alternatively, if planning to borrow the initial finance, there will be a surplus of £10 after the loan has been repaid. If the project were risk-free and the net cash flows certain, then the investment would be undertaken, in the absence of a better one.

The calculation of the internal rate of return

Instead of considering the expected net present value of a project, an alternative approach is to calculate the actual rate of return which it yields. Future net cash flows are estimated in the same way as in the example above, but instead of discounting them by the rate of interest, the potential investor calculates the rate which, when used to discount them, exactly equates the summed net cash flows of the project with its initial cost that is, makes the $NPV = 0$. This may be expressed as follows:

$$0 = R_0 + R_1/(1 + i) + R_2/(1 + i)^2 + \cdots + R_n/(1 + i)^n$$

where R = the real return or net cash flow, having allowed for inflation in the period concerned
i = the internal rate of return.

As before, R_0 includes the cost of the project and will therefore usually be a negative number. Using the previous example but now allowing R_0 = £300, yields:

$$0 = - £300 + 110/(1 + i) + 121/(1 + i)^2 + 133/(1 + i)^3$$

It follows therefore that the value of i which solves the equation is 0.1 or 10 per cent.

The calculation of the internal rate of return is often problematic, even if the requisite information on future costs and revenues is available. For instance there is not always a unique value of i for which the net present value $=0$. While these problems are beyond the scope of this book, it is still important to understand the basic concept of the calculation of a rate of return on investment.

The internal rate of return is then compared with the market rate of interest. The investor will undertake the project with the highest rate of return, assuming this is above the prevailing rate of interest. The internal rate of return is often referred to as the *Marginal efficiency of capital* (*MEC*) because in the aggregate, assuming no risk, it would be expected that the stock of capital in an economy would adjust until the internal rate of return of the marginal project would be equal to the ruling rate of interest. In one sense people would continue to borrow money for capital formation as long as there were projects which promised a return which at least paid for the loan. In another, people with funds to invest would use them for capital formation while this promised to yield a higher rate of return than the rate of interest. This implies a marginal efficiency of capital schedule which defines the desired capital stock in an economy in terms of the rate of interest, as shown in Figure 2.6 where K = desired capital stock.

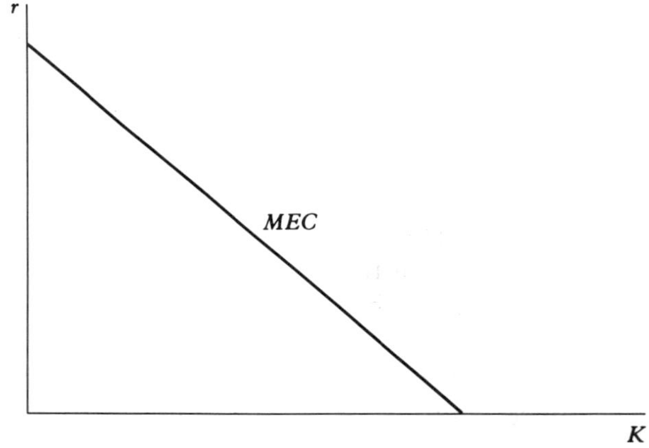

Figure 2.6 *The marginal efficiency of capital schedule*

The various possible investment projects that can be undertaken are ranked in descending order according to their expected internal rate of return. The market rate of interest acts as a cut-off point in that there is no desire to undertake projects which yield a lower rate of return. This analysis implies a key role played by the rate of interest in determining the level of desired capital stock in an economy.

It is important to make a clear distinction between capital and investment. Capital refers to the stock of plant and machinery, buildings, roads, etc., at any single point in time. Net investment refers to changes in the size of the stock through time, and therefore refers to a flow of activity. It would appear that higher rates of interest should be associated with lower levels of investment as fewer of the projects available would be undertaken.

In reality the situation is far more complicated. First, changes in the rate of interest would affect the demand for capital goods and services which, all other things being equal, would be expected to affect their price. This means, in effect, that the initial cost of the project has changed and so therefore has its internal rate of return; the same expected future net cash flows are equated with a different cost, so the rate of discount which exactly equates them must be different. Likewise if the initial cost has altered the *NPV* will also be affected. To follow the implications of this dynamic process is beyond the scope of this text. For the purposes of this analysis it is sufficient to observe that the points above imply an inverse relationship between interest rates and the level of investment. To understand how stable or unstable this relationship might be, it is necessary to consider some of the other influences upon the investment decision. One potential source of volatility which Keynes considered to be of major importance was that of expectations and uncertainty.

EXPECTATIONS AND UNCERTAINTY

The considerable role which these play in the investment decision is probably best demonstrated by a reconsideration of the discounting process described above. This involves the calculation of the expected net cash flows in each of the time periods over which the project is to run, and the application to these of a discount rate. In the case of the net present value, the rate used is the market rate of interest. In the case of the internal rate of return, the investor is actually solving the calculation to find the discount rate which, when applied to the expected net cash flows equates their sum with the initial cost of the project; this is then compared to the rate of interest. The apparently pre-eminent role played by the rate of interest in this investment decision tends to distract attention from the nature of the calculation of expected net cash flows. This calculation is often extremely difficult and uncertain.

Consider the information required to estimate such flows. The expected net cash flow from a project in a given time period t is equal to the expected revenues accrued minus the expected costs incurred in the same period.

In order to calculate expected cost, the potential investor must estimate a variety of different costs according to the nature of the production process. These might typically include, for example, forecasts of labour costs, land rents, power, fuel and other overheads. Raw material costs would also require estimation, and if any reliance is placed upon imports of these then a forecast of their cost implies some assumption or prediction of exchange rates. Unless the project under consideration is of very short duration, these forecasts may be very difficult to make. Under the present regime of floating exchange rates, for example, both governments and professional forecasters find it extremely difficult to forecast very far into the future with much confidence. The expected lifetime of any investment in capital formation dictates to a large extent the period over which such forecasts must be made; many individuals, firms and indeed governments may find themselves required to make predictions for long periods into the future.

In order to calculate expected revenues it is necessary to forecast the two components involved, price and quantity. Any forecast of quantity sold implies an assumption as to the price commanded, as the two are so closely interrelated. Given a specific price, there are still many problems in predicting the quantity which is expected to be sold at some point in the future. These arise because the demand for a product is determined by many other factors apart from price. Examples of some of the other variables which affect demand are income, taste, prices and marketing of competing products. Some of these will in turn be affected by the behaviour of the investor. The pricing and marketing strategies adopted by the potential investor would be expected to have some effect upon those of his competitors. Clearly, to take into account all of these interrelated factors would be impractical in most cases and some relatively crude assumptions are made to enable any prediction of future revenues.

The problems associated with forecasting tend to be greater, the further into the future one attempts to predict. To understand how the estimates of future net cash flows are affected by these problems it is necessary to distinguish between *expectations* and *uncertainty*. Expectations describe what people expect to happen in the future, given the information available to them. Uncertainty refers to the extent to which they trust, or have confidence in, these expectations. For example, a firm in the 1960s would have been more certain or confident about its expectations with respect to future exchange rates than one involved in the prediction in the late 1980s, because the 1960s rates were fixed within very tight limits as opposed to floating relatively freely in the 1980s.

The final estimate of *R*, the return or net cash flow in some future time period, is arrived at by taking the expectations of the various factors involved and then adjusting them according to the degree of uncertainty felt by the investor. In general, the more uncertain people are as to the accuracy of their expectations the more 'conservative' they will be in terms of the estimates which they actually include in the discounting process; costs will be revised upwards, and revenues downwards. The resulting value of *R* is squeezed from both directions in the event of a rise in 'uncertainty'. The importance of this in the investment decision depends on the sensitivity of investors to increased uncertainty.

In times of greater uncertainty potential investors will often raise the discount rate which they use and/or reduce the assumed 'economic' life of the project concerned.

These factors of expectations and uncertainty help to explain the potential volatility of aggregate investment demand with respect to the rate of interest. The whole *MEC* schedule, as described above, is shifted either up or down by changes in people's expectations or the degree of certainty with which they hold them. It is not surprising that the actual investment decisions which result from these fluctations in the desired capital stock appear to be unrelated to changes in the market rate of interest.

THE RATE OF CHANGE OF INCOME AND THE 'ACCELERATOR PRINCIPLE'

In general, different levels of production require different amounts of capital. If income is changing, so is the demand for production and through it the demand for investment goods and services. In order to understand the determinants of investment resulting from changes in income, it is helpful to reiterate the distinction between *gross* and *net* investment. *Gross investment* refers to the total production of goods and services to enable production; it therefore includes replacement capital to counter the effects of depreciation. *Net investment* refers to changes in the size of the employed stock of capital; it can therefore take a positive or negative value, If, for example, the level of gross investment is less than the amount of plant and machinery which has been scrapped in an economy, then the actual capital stock has shrunk and the productive capacity is reduced. There has been negative net investment despite positive gross investment.

Consider the case of a steady increase in demand due to rising income. The stock of capital rises to meet this increase in demand. The amount by which it rises is determined by the *capital–output ratio.* This refers to the number of pounds' worth of plant and machinery required to produce one pound's worth of output in a given time period such as one year. If it is assumed that, on average, it requires three pounds' worth of capital formation to produce one pound's worth of output in a year, then the amount of investment in additional capital will need to be three times the value of the increase in demand. It should be remembered that capital formation creates the potential to produce over a number of years and that this will vary according to the type of product and its means of production. This explains why, on average, the capital–output ratio is greater than one, because only one year's output is being considered. The point here is that in order to satisfy an increase in effective demand, the stock of capital must rise by three times the amount of the increase: the increase in demand has an accelerated effect upon net investment. The accelerator in this example is three, which is the capital–output ratio.

The full implications of this accelerator effect in practice are clearly demonstrated by a simple example which considers the case of a single firm. Assume that this firm uses machines which are each capable of producing ten units of output every year for ten years, after which they are useless. The firm has ten machines which it has bought at the rate of one a year over the previous ten years. In the eleventh year demand for the product rises by a further 10 per cent to 110 units. Instead of ordering just one machine to expand output, the firm must also buy a replacement for the oldest machine which is now useless. A 10 per cent increase in demand for the product has led to a 100 per cent rise in investment demand.

In effect this implies that any increase in effective demand will cause a greater, or accelerated, rise in investment. In practice the extent to which this occurs will depend upon industry's capacity to increase production through the more intensive use of the capital which it already has at its disposal.

This accelerator effect upon investment can also be negative. Consider the case of a reduction in the demand for the product in the example above, of 10 per cent. The firm no longer needs to replace the worn out machine in order to meet the demand for its product. It has thus reduced its investment demand by 100 per cent.

Changes in the level of income and the resultant changes in demand will therefore tend to affect the level of investment. In theory net investment will be some multiple of the change in demand which has brought it about. In practice the strength of the effect will depend upon several factors. It will be smaller if there is unused capacity available in the capital stock, or if the change in demand is correctly judged to be short term and is met out of stocks.

THE LEVEL OF INCOME

While the rate of change of income affects net investment it would be expected that, in general, different levels would affect gross investment through the level of scrapping and its replacement. Consider the case of a constant level of income: there will be no net investment because the amount of capital employed is not required to change to meet a different level of output. Gross investment will be equal to the volume of capital goods and services which have been consumed, or ceased to be effective, in the previous period. This will tend to be larger at higher levels of income because more capital is employed and, if it is assumed that income and demand have been constant for a long time, more capital will become exhausted. Despite some simplifying assumptions it is clear that higher levels of output will tend to be associated with more investment for replacement purposes.

TECHNOLOGICAL PROGRESS

Technological progress affects investment demand in a variety of ways. It is sufficient here to restrict consideration to two main effects. First, it may enable the production of completely new types of goods or services and render the production of earlier versions unprofitable. This may introduce more potential investment projects, some of which will attract investment because they are expected to yield a sufficiently high return. There may therefore be a net increase in the number of investment projects which are deemed viable, given prevailing interest rates, expectations and uncertainty. Second, technological progress may shorten the economic life of employed capital by rendering it unprofitable before its production capacity has been reduced by age. In this event firms may be required to upgrade some of their plant and machinery, for example, in order to remain competitive with other firms which have already done so. In order to remain viable, firms may be forced to adopt new capital which reduces production costs, despite the fact that their present system of production is still operative.

Both of these effects imply that more rapid technological progress will lead to additional investment. As a result of this there may also be further increases in investment in research and development to enable technological progress and, for those concerned, the ability to take advantage of it earlier.

To summarize, the level of private investment demand is determined by many factors, of which the main ones have been discussed briefly above. In theory individuals and firms will continue investing in plant and machinery while the expected return is greater than the prevailing rate of interest. In terms of microeconomic theory they will attempt to maximize profits by investing up to the point where the marginal cost of such investment is equal to the expected marginal revenue.

Government demand

The third element of aggregate demand arises from the activities of government. In part, as was explained in the section on consumption above, it is the variation of this constituent of aggregate demand which Keynesians believe is crucial to manipulating and managing the overall level of economic activity.

Government demand consists of consumption and investment expenditures in many areas of the economy to provide, for example, education, health services, defence, communications, etc. This demand also arises from governments' direct involvement in industry through the nationalized industries and also indirectly through regional and industrial policies to aid and influence the private sector. In addition, governments provide a complex system of transfer payments which provide the recipients with an income in the absence of a corresponding contribution to production. Examples of such transfer payments are state pensions and the provision of unemployment benefit and social security.

A detailed description and analysis of this aspect of government activity is not appropriate here. It would be a mistake to assume, however, that the level of expenditure simply reflects the priorities which governments believe to be desirable. Given an accepted set of transfer payments, the actual level of expenditure involved is determined by the number of qualifying recipients. Governments can specify the level of benefits which can be claimed by the unemployed, but they have far less control over the actual number of bona fide claimants. There is a considerable element of inertia in the determination of government expenditure which makes the task of demand management both problematic and highly imperfect.

The actual determinants of government demand are therefore highly complex and ever changing, particularly given their necessary political overtones. Since government expenditure is funded through taxation and borrowing, constraints upon both of these sources of revenue will also determine to some extent the actual level of expenditure which is considered feasible. Changes in the relative levels of government expenditure and taxation constitute fiscal policy.

Trade

The overall level of aggregate demand also includes the balance of trade, the difference in total value between exported and imported goods and services. This was represented earlier in the chapter as $(X - M)$ and can take a positive or negative value. The balance of trade constitutes that part of the balance of payments referred to as the *current account*; the other side is the *capital account*.

The *current* account refers to the sale and purchase of currencies in order to enable the purchase of imported and exported goods and services. These represent the purchases of 'visible' goods and 'invisible' services. The purchase of a foreign product requires the purchaser to buy the foreign currency concerned, in an amount sufficient to pay the supplier in its country of origin. The purchase of a 'visible' product like a car, for example, or an 'invisible' product like insurance, can only occur between countries if they make the requisite currency transactions.

Taking the UK as an example, a surplus on current account arises if the volume of foreign currencies offered in exchange for pounds sterling, to purchase UK exports, exceeds that of pounds to exchange for foreign currencies to purchase imports: the value of exports exceeds that of imports. A deficit on current account exists in the reverse situation as manifested by a shortage rather than a surplus of foreign currencies offered for sterling.

The *capital* account refers to the sale and purchase of currency in order to enable an investment in another country or to increase or deplete a country's reserves of foreign currencies. Flows of currency which occur, for example, in response to changes in relative interest rates between countries are recorded as debits (outflows) or credits (inflows) on the capital account. As with the case of the current account, a surplus on the capital account is reflected in a surplus of foreign currencies being offered for sterling to invest in UK industry or financial assets. The opposite is true in the case of a deficit.

International capital flows reflect the movement of funds in pursuit of the highest return; it would be expected that, all other things being unchanged, they would therefore reflect relative interest rates between countries. Funds would tend to move towards countries with relatively higher rates.

Since all currency sold must have been purchased, it is clear that the overall balance of payments is always in balance; a deficit on one account must be balanced by a surplus on the other. If the value of imports exceeds that of exports (a deficit on current account) then there must either be a net inflow of foreign currencies for investment purposes, or the reserves of foreign currencies will fall and those of sterling rise (a surplus on capital account).

As concern here is with the contribution of the current account to the level of aggregate demand it is important to consider three interrelated factors that determine the balance in value between exports and imports:

(*a*) The exchange rate
(*b*) Relative prices
(*c*) The level of disposable income

THE EXCHANGE RATE

The rate at which the domestic currency exchanges for foreign currencies determines the relative prices of exports and imports in their respective markets. It therefore determines both the relative competitiveness of exports in markets abroad and imports in the domestic economy. Given a particular volume of exports and imports, the exchange rate also defines their absolute value, according to the prices set by exporters and importers in terms of their own currencies.

RELATIVE PRICES

In the absence of exchange rate variations, the level of exports and imports will vary according to changes in relative prices between trading countries. Countries which experience relatively more rapid price inflation will, all other things remaining equal, experience a fall in price competitiveness in both foreign and domestic markets. Their exports will become less competitive abroad while imports will be increasingly competitive in the home market. If these relative price variations are perfectly accommodated in exchange rate changes, then differences in price competitiveness are eliminated.

THE LEVEL OF DISPOSABLE INCOME

In terms of the domestic economy, the demand for imports will also be affected by the level of income and economic activity. Increases in the amount of disposable income will raise the demand for imported goods and services for a given set of relative prices in the domestic market. Similarly, higher levels of production may require larger quantities of imported goods and services for the production process itself.

In summary, the contribution of the net trade balance to aggregate demand is determined by many factors, both exogenous and endogenous to the economy. The particular mixture of external and internal factors is difficult if not impossible to predict with any confidence, thus adding further difficulties to the task of aggregate demand management.

Additional reading

THE CONSUMPTION FUNCTION

1. Duesenberry, J. S. (1949) *Income, Saving and the Theory of Consumption Behaviour*, Harvard University Press.
2. Friedman, M. (1957) *A Theory of the Consumption Function*, Princeton University Press. (Chapters 1–3, 6, 9.)
3. Keynes, J. M. (1936) *The General Theory of Employment, Interest, and Money*, Macmillan. (Chapters 8 and 9.)

THE INVESTMENT FUNCTION

1. Eisner, R. 'A Permanent Income Theory for Investment'. *American Economic Review*, June 1967.
2. Hawkins, C. and Pearce, I. (1971) *Capital Investment Appraisal*, Macmillan.
3. Keynes, J. M. (1936) *The General Theory of Employment, Interest, and Money*, Macmillan. (Book IV.)

4. Knox, A. D. 'The Acceleration Principle and the Theory of Investment: A Survey' in M. G. Mueller, *Readings in Macroeconomics*, 2nd edn, Holt International, 1971. (This book contains a number of relevant collected papers.)

3.

Investment and saving: The *IS* schedule

Having examined the constituents of aggregate demand, it is possible to observe and illustrate one of the fundamental differences between the Classical and Keynesian models. This concerns the way in which investment and saving are made equal and the implication this has for the level of national income.

Consider the simple closed economy, where there is no foreign trade, no government and hence no taxation. In this case the only elements of aggregate demand are consumption and investment expenditures. Thus:

$$Y = C + I$$

This equation expresses national income in terms of the expenditures made on consumption and investment goods. Reference back to Figure 2.1 shows that another way of considering income is in terms of the production that it implies, and in turn in terms of the payments received by the factors involved in that production.

If the definition of investment is widened to include the stock of finished but unsold goods held by firms, then it follows that over any given period total expenditure is equal to total production and both are equal to the level of national income. The expenditures made on consumption and investment goods will eventually be received by the factors of production responsible in the form of either wages, salaries, rents, interest and profit. The equation $Y = C + I$ thus represents three different ways of measuring national income or aggregate demand; namely as expenditure, the value production, or payments made to factors of production. The payments received by factors of production as income may be either spent on consumption or saved. Income is therefore equal to the sum of consumption and saving.

$$Y = C + S$$

where S = saving. If $Y = C + S$ and $Y = C + I$, then it follows that S and I must be equal when income is in equilibrium. The debate concerns how savings and investment are brought into equality.

According to the Classical school, any discrepancy between the levels of investment and saving is rectified by changes in the rate of interest. The rate of interest reflects the cost of borrowing funds for investment purposes and also the reward for deferring current consumption. If businesses demand a higher level of funds for investment purposes this will, other things being equal, raise the cost of those funds. The interest rate will rise. The effect is also to raise the cost of current consumption, in that a higher rate of return on saved income must now be forgone in order to consume out of current income. Economists refer to the notion of valuing a resource, in this case income, in terms of its alternative use as the *opportunity cost* of that resource. Thus the opportunity cost of using income for current consumption has risen. This will induce individuals to save a greater proportion of their income, the process continuing until the supply and demand for loanable funds is again equal, but at a higher rate of interest. The opposite would be true for a fall in investment demand.

Keynesians believe that investment and saving are equated by changes in both the rate of interest and the level of income. Since consumption is a function of income, and income is itself equal to the sum of consumption and saving, it follows that saving must also be a function of income. The determination and role of the rate of interest requires a discussion of the supply of and demand for money; this is deferred until the following chapter, so that concentration can be focused on the equilibrating influence of income changes in the Keynesian model. Central to this theme is the concept of the *national income multiplier*.

The national income multiplier

Income is a flow of economic activity in which there are both leakages and injections in terms of the demand for that activity. In this simple closed economy investment is the only injection and savings the only leakage. According to the multiplier principle a change in investment will have a multiplied effect upon the equilibrium level of income. Consider the effect of an increase in investment due to more optimistic expectations. This is received as income by those involved in the production of the capital goods and services concerned. From the simple consumption function described earlier, $C = a + bY$, a proportion of this income b is spent upon consumption. Those involved in the production of these consumption goods and services will in turn receive these expenditures as income themselves. They will also, on average, spend the same proportion of this income on consumption and this expenditure will be received as income by the producers of those goods and services, and so the process continues. The original increase in investment has served to increase income by that amount, plus the consumption effect. The overall size of the consumption effect is determined by the *MPC*. The greater this is, the larger the consumption effect, because more of the income received at each stage in the process is respent on consumption and thus received as income to be respent or saved.

If investment increases by £1000 and the proportion of any increase in income which is spent upon consumption, the *MPC*, is 4/5 or 80 per cent, then the eventual effect upon income will be as follows:

£1000 + (0.8) £1000 + (0.8) × (0.8) £1000, etc., or:
£1000 + £800 + £640 . . .

If the *MPC* is b, then another way of expressing this would be as follows:

$$£1000 + b \times £1000 + b \times b \times £1000 + b \times b \times b\, £1000 \ldots$$

Income is increasing at each stage, but by an ever diminishing amount (the exception being the case where the $MPC = 1$: all the increase in income is respent at each step, and income rises to infinity). The actual sum of this series can be expressed as a ratio of the eventual increase in income to the initial change in injections, in this case investment, as follows:

$$\Delta Y/\Delta I = 1/(1-b)$$

where ΔY = the eventual increase in income and ΔI = the change in investment.

This can be demonstrated algebraically as follows:

$$Y = C + I; \qquad C = a + bY$$
$$Y = a + bY + I$$
$$\Delta Y = b\Delta Y + \Delta I \qquad \text{because } a \text{ is a fixed quantity}$$
$$(1-b)\Delta Y = \Delta I$$
$$\Delta Y/\Delta I = 1/(1-b)$$

If $b = 0.8$ then $\Delta Y/\Delta I = 5$ and so the multiplier is equal to 5.

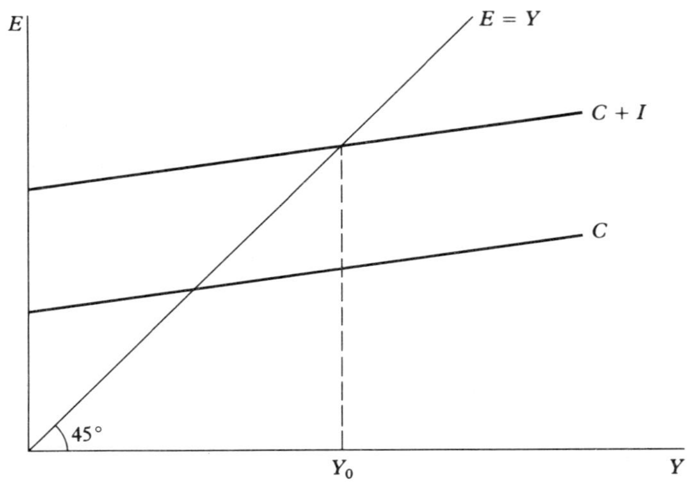

Figure 3.1 *The equilibrium level of income*

For a graphical explanation it is necessary to return to the consumption function and add the increase in investment at each level of income, as in Figure 3.1. This results in a line, above and parallel to the consumption function, because it is assumed in this simple model that different levels of income do not cause different levels of investment.

The importance of the 45 degree line is now clear: it represents equilibria in the 'real' or goods and services market because, along the line, planned expenditure is equal to income. Consumption and investment expenditure are shown on the vertical axis, and the level of income is given on the horizontal axis. The multiplier effect of an increase in investment can be seen in Figure 3.2.

As total expenditure rises from $C + I_0$ *to* $C + I_1$, income rises from Y_0 to Y_1; the increase in income ΔY is larger than the change in investment ΔI which brought it about; the exception being the case where a change in income has no effect upon consumption, equivalent to an *MPC* of zero. The multiplier effect exists given a positive marginal propensity to consume, and its size is determined by that value.

As consumption is determined by income in this simple economy so, by definition, is saving. If at each stage 80 per cent of income is spent on consumption, then 20 per cent of it is saved. Through the multiplier effect income rises by five times the original increase in investment, leading to a rise in saving by 20 per cent of that rise in income; investment and saving are again equal. In the example above, the rise in

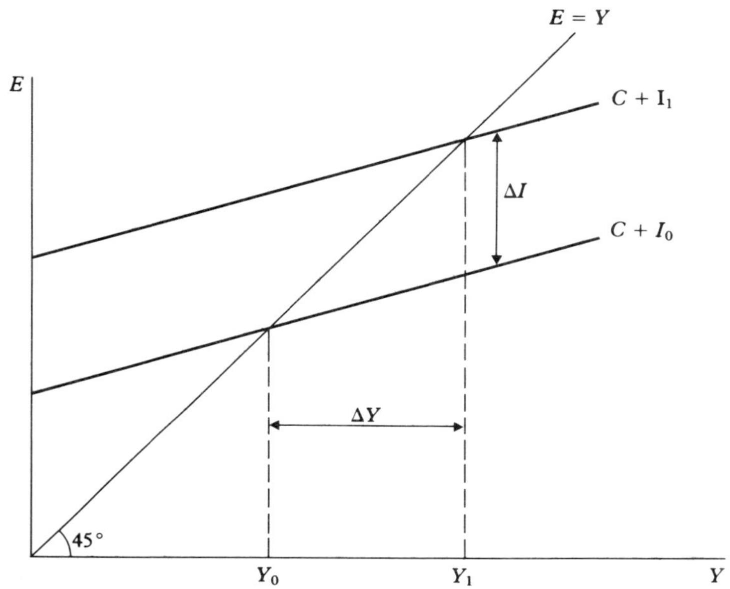

Figure 3.2 *The multiplier effect*

investment of £1000 causes income to rise by £5000 through the multiplier, thus inducing an increase in saving of £1000.

If the model was extended to include a government sector, its expenditure would constitute an additional injection into, and taxation an additional withdrawal from, the income flow. The effect would be to reduce the size of the multiplier because now, at each round of expenditure induced by the investment change, an amount of income would leak away through taxation in addition to that which is saved. Algebraically:

$$Y = C + I + G$$
$$C = a + b(Y - T)$$

where T = taxes.
If taxes are related to income, we may write T as

$$T = tY$$

where t = the tax rate; t may be interpreted as the rate of income tax such that $t = 0.2$ would indicate a tax rate of 20 per cent. Thus:

$C = a + b(Y - tY)$
$Y = a + b(Y - tY) + I + G$

Allowing investment to change

$\Delta Y = b(\Delta Y - t\Delta Y) + \Delta I$

where G and a drop out as constants and hence

$$\Delta Y(1 - b + bt) = \Delta I$$
$$\Delta Y = \Delta I/(1 - b + bt)$$
$$\Delta Y/\Delta I = 1/(1 - b + bt)$$

and $1/(1 - b + bt) < 1/(1 - b)$
given $0 \leqslant t \leqslant 1$.

In general an additional withdrawal reduces the size of the multiplier effect. Thus the extension of the above to include trade would also reduce the size of the multiplier, because import expenditure is an outflow or leakage from the income flow. Exactly similar expressions could be derived for a change in government expenditure or export income.

The *IS* schedule

The *IS* schedule refers to levels of income and rates of interest which correspond to equilibrium in the market for goods and services. To return to a simple format, the equilibrium level of income may be expressed as:

$Y = C + S$ all incomes are spent on consumption, or saved.
or $Y = C + I$ all real income is composed of goods and services, either for consumption or investment.

In equilibrium, planned saving and investment are equal: their equality is brought about for any given level of investment through changes in income by the multiplier process. A rise in investment causes the requisite rise in income to create an increase in savings equal to the original injection of investment demand. Higher levels of investment correspond to higher levels of income and thus higher levels of saving.

From the simple model of investment described above, lower rates of interest are associated with higher levels of investment. For equilibrium in the goods market it would be expected that lower rates of

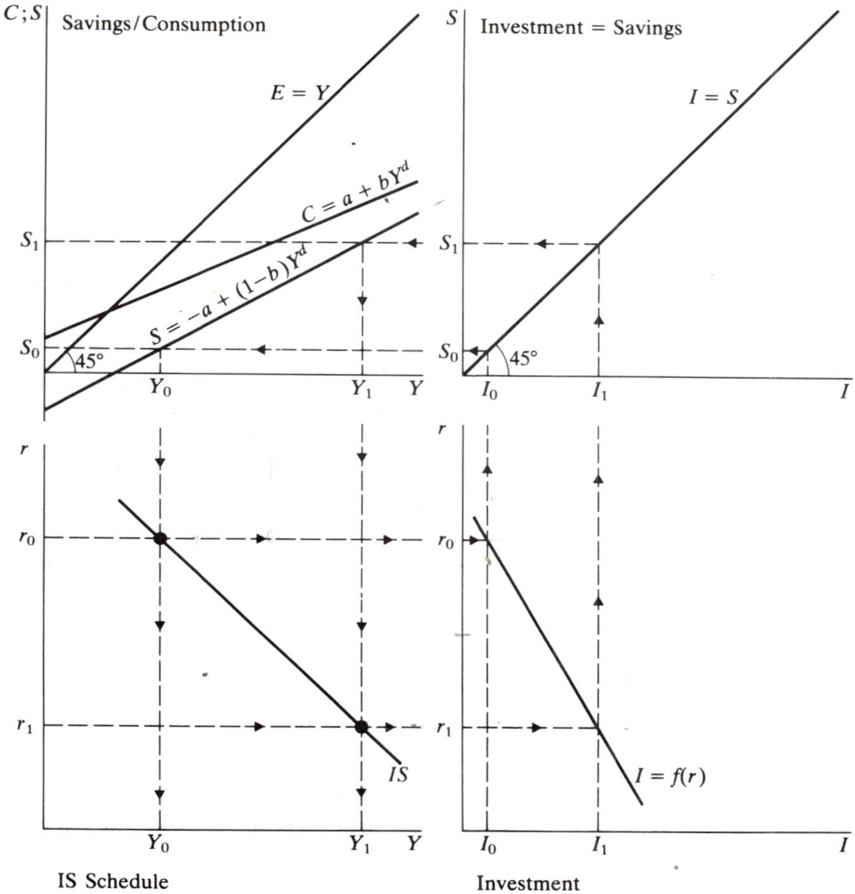

Figure 3.3 *The derivation of the* IS *schedule*

interest should correspond to the higher levels of income necessary to provide the appropriate level of savings. This can be demonstrated as shown in Figure 3.3.

Starting at interest rate r_0 the level of investment is I_0. From the consumption function, $C = a + bY^d$, the savings function, $S = -a + (1 - b)Y^d$, can be derived from the condition $Y = C + S$. Given these functions, it is clear that the level of income which equates investment and savings is Y_0; $r_0 Y_0$ is therefore on the *IS* schedule. The lower rate of interest r_1 leads to a higher level of investment I_1 which through the multiplier creates a higher level of income Y_1, thus illustrating a further combination r_1, Y_1; the *IS* schedule therefore slopes downwards from left to right. It can be seen from the diagram that the slope of the *IS* curve must be determined by the slopes of the consumption and investment functions. For example, the greater the *MPC*, the steeper the consumption function, and thus the flatter will be the *IS* schedule. An increase in the *MPC* makes the multiplier larger: the level of investment associated with any given rate of interest will have a larger impact upon the equilibrium level of income. Thus each rate of interest is associated with a higher level of income making the *IS* schedule flatter.

The less sensitive investment is to the rate of interest, the steeper the investment function, which leads to a steeper *IS* schedule. Any given change in the rate of interest will have a smaller effect upon investment and hence, through the multiplier, a smaller effect on income. If a given movement in the interest rate is to be associated with smaller variations in income, the *IS* curve must become steeper.

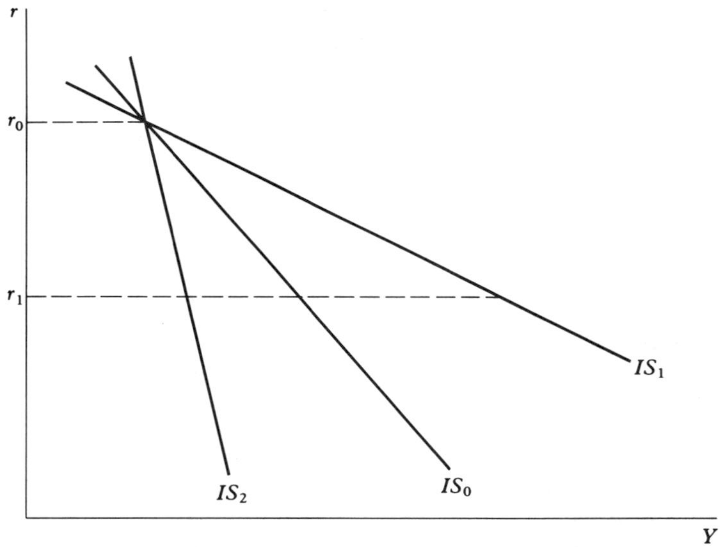

Figure 3.4 *The* IS *schedule with changes in slope*

If IS_0 corresponds to that derived in Figure 3.3, then IS_1 would result from an increase in the *MPC*, and IS_2 from a reduction in the sensitivity of investment to the rate of interest. The implications for the equilibrium level of income at r_1 are clear.

Conversely a fall in the *MPC*, that is, an increase in the desire to save, will steepen the IS schedule (IS_0 to IS_2) and an increase in the sensitivity of investment to variations in the rate of interest will flatten the schedule (IS_0 to IS_1).

The inclusion of government

Extending the model to include the role of government introduces the elements of government expenditure and taxation.

Consider an increase in government expenditure on goods and services, all other things being equal; this acts as an injection into the income flow and raises the level of income via the multiplier effect. There is at this stage no reason to expect this to influence the rate of interest or level of investment. The result, therefore, is that each rate of interest is associated with a higher level of injections, namely, the relevant level of investment and the new level of government purchases, and so a higher level of income. The result is that the IS curve shifts outwards to the right, the new curve being parallel to the previous one. By a similar argument a reduction in government expenditures would cause the IS curve to shift backwards to the left.

A change in taxation revenue will, other things being equal, change the net expenditure of government. If the government reduces the general level of taxation, its net expenditure is increased. In the case of a lump sum tax, the effect is identical to that described above, because there is no effect on the multiplier relationship. In the case of an income tax change, however, the multiplier relationship *will* be altered. In the case of a reduction in income tax, the multiplier effect becomes larger and so each rate of interest will be associated with a higher level of income. The IS schedule becomes flatter and moves outwards to the right. Conversely, an increase in taxation will shift the IS schedule backwards and also steepen the curve because of the reduction in the size of the multiplier. Each level of injections, investment and government expenditures leads, through a smaller multiplier effect, to a lower level of equilibrium income. These effects are demonstrated in Figure 3.5.

Figure 3.5(a) shows the parallel shift induced by a change in government expenditure or lump sum taxes. Figure 3.5(b) illustrates the income tax effects on IS. At an initial tax rate t_0, IS is at position IS_0. If the tax rate t_0 is raised to t_1, the curve rotates backwards to IS_1. A reduction in the tax rate to t_0 would rotate the curve back to the right to position IS_0.

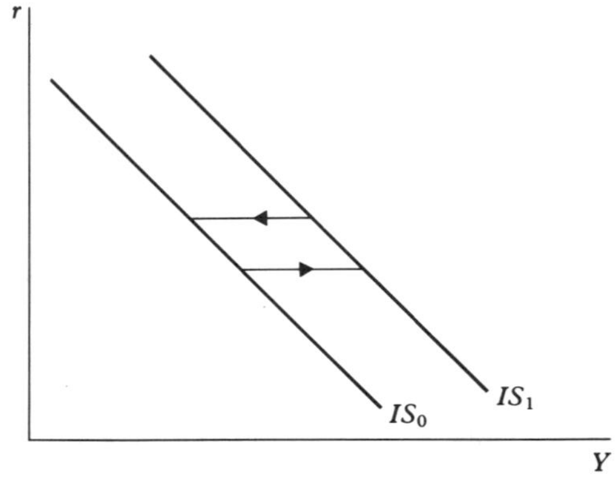

(a) Expenditure changes and lump sum tax

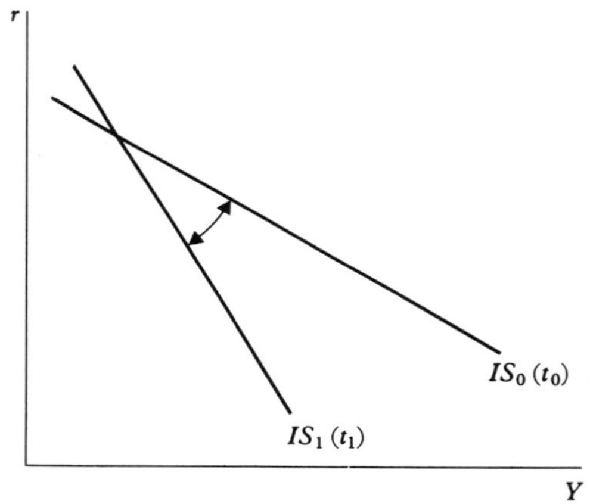

(b) Income tax changes

Figure 3.5 *The role of government and the* IS *schedule*

Similar implications to those described for government tax-rate and expenditure changes also hold for changes in the level of exports and the propensity to import. Exports act as an additional injection, shifting *IS* parallel, while imports constitute an additional withdrawal. Given that import demand is a function of income, the desire to purchase imported goods will affect the multiplier. An increase in the marginal propensity to import (*MPI*) has similar effects to an increase in the tax rate, rotating the *IS* schedule backwards to the left. Likewise a reduction in the *MPI* acts in the same way as a reduction in the tax rate.

Variations in the gradient and position of the *IS* schedule have important policy implications in the Keynesian model which are discussed in Chapter 5.

Additional reading

In addition to all the good modern macroeconomic texts the reader may wish to look at:

1. Hicks, J. R., 'Mr Keynes and the "Classics"; A Suggested Interpretation', in M. G. Mueller, *Readings in Macroeconomics*, 2nd edn, Holt International, 1971.

4.

Money and the rate of interest: The *LM* schedule

The demand for money

In order to explain how the demand for and the supply of money are equated under the Classical and Keynesian assumptions, it is necessary to define what money is. The definition of money is determined by the degree of 'liquidity' which is assumed, that is, the ease with which it can be used as a means of transaction. In its purest or most liquid sense, money is cash, notes and coins. Non-interest-bearing current bank accounts may also be included as, to all intents and purposes, these are also perfectly liquid for most transactions, given a stable banking system. In attempting to measure the money supply, governments use a variety of measures, each of which corresponds to a different level of liquidity. The lowest level of measurement is M0, and refers to cash, notes and coinage. M1 is the amount of cash in circulation plus current bank accounts; many other measures of the money supply are possible. For the purposes of this analysis, it is sufficient to assume that money is M1.

THE CLASSICAL VIEW

In the Classical system, money is only demanded as a means of exchange. The Classical interpretation of the role of money rests upon the so-called *quantity theory of money*. This is expressed as follows:

$$MV = PT$$

where M = the demand for money
V = the velocity of circulation of money
P = the average price level
T = the number of transactions

MV represents the amount of money and its rate of usage, while PT

refers to the average price of transactions multiplied by the number of transactions made, which is equivalent to the level of money income.

The velocity of circulation is defined as the average number of times that £1 changes hands over a given time period. Assuming this to be constant, the quantity theory can be restated as:

$M = 1/V \times PT$ or
$M = c \times PT$

The demand for money, *M*, is proportionately related to the level of money income. If the money supply is increased in the absence of any increase in transactions, or real income, then there must be a proportionate increase in the average price level to retain the equality of money supply and demand. It is this relationship which underlies many governments' attempts to control price inflation through the money supply. Under this system, the demand for and the supply of money are equated by changes in money income, either through changes in the average price level or in the level of real income. Under the assumptions of Classical macroeconomic theory the rate of interest is determined by the supply and demand of loan finance; it is not affected directly by changes in the supply and demand for money itself.

THE KEYNESIAN VIEW

In order to perceive the main theoretical innovation which Keynes introduced to the money economy, it is necessary to consider the components of the demand for money itself. Consider the demand for money as a means of exchange; this can be divided into two motives: the *transactions* and *precautionary demands.*

Individuals, households and firms hold money balances in order to make *transactions.* The need for these balances arises because receipts and payments of money are not synchronized. For example, wages are usually paid once a week while payments for goods and services are made each day. The amount of money which is held for this purpose will depend upon the real value of transactions, or real income, and the extent to which payments and receipts are unsynchronized. If the latter is assumed to be constant, then this demand for money will be directly related to the former, the level of real income.

The *precautionary motive* for holding money arises because the pattern of transactions is not perfectly anticipated. Additional balances are held in order to enable payments which are not predicted exactly. The extent to which money is demanded for this purpose is primarily determined by two influences: the level of real income and the rate of interest. The amount of money which is considered necessary to cover unanticipated purchases will tend to rise with the number of purchases made. The rate of interest represents the opportunity cost of holding money in that it is the return forgone by not lending it at that rate. The higher the rate of interest, the lower the demand for precautionary balances. If it is assumed, to simplify the analysis, that these balances are solely determined by the level of income, then they can be added in with the transactions balance to give the demand for *active* money balances (*Mda*) as shown in Figure 4.1.

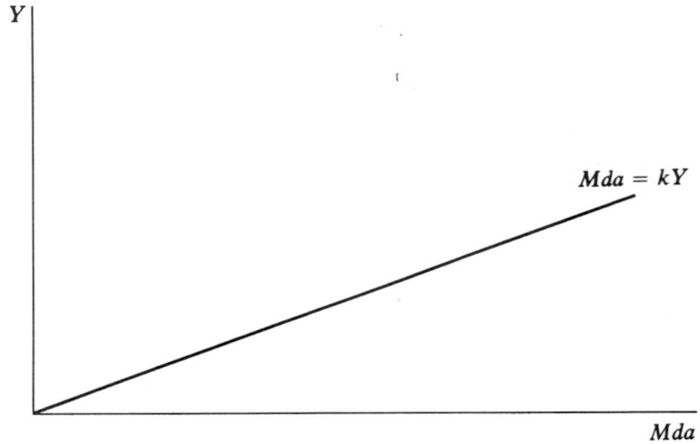

Figure 4.1 *The demand for active money balances*

In its simplest form, the Classical interpretation of the demand for money finishes here. Money is only held to enable the purchase of goods and services. Keynes introduced an additional motive for the holding of money balances, based upon the idea that money itself yielded utility over and above that which it represented in terms of the value of the goods and services which it could be used to purchase. He believed that money is also demanded because of its perfect liquidity: it provides the holder with the ability to enter into any market transaction immediately. There is, according to this view, a demand or preference for money simply because it is the most versatile means of exchange.

Liquidity preference

The concept of *liquidity preference* provides the third motive for holding money; it is held as one constituent in portfolios of financial assets in order to enable instant participation in the markets for interest-bearing assets, i.e., it is part of a store of wealth. To simplify for the purpose of clarity, consider the case of portfolios containing just money and fixed-interest-bearing government bonds.

The ratio of money to bonds which people choose is determined by their expectations of the market rate of interest. If they expect this to rise, they will reduce bond holdings and demand more money and vice versa. To understand why this occurs, it is necessary to consider the nature of bonds in more detail. The bonds concerned have a fixed money yield. For example, if they were issued at a time when the prevailing rate was 10 per cent and they constituted a loan to the government of £100, then the bearer receives £10 each year from the government until the bonds 'mature'. (Some governments in the past raised money by issuing bonds with no maturity date which simply yielded a fixed nominal amount to the holder in perpetuity.) Changes in the market rate of interest have no effect on the absolute amount which is paid to the bond holder. This means that if the holder wishes, for any reason, to sell the bonds, the price achieved will depend upon the market rate of interest. The bonds will only be worth £100 to someone else, if this rate is 10 per cent. If it were 20 per cent, the bond would only sell for £50 to bring its yield in line with alternative financial assets. Bond prices change in response to changes in the rate of interest, because the money return which they provide is fixed in absolute terms. They are inversely related, because higher rates of interest require lower bond prices for the yield to represent the higher percentage of that price.

The balance between money and bonds which holders choose is therefore based, in a sense, upon what they speculate will happen to the rate of interest. If they expect it to rise, they will reduce bond holdings in preference for money because they expect bond prices to fall as a result. If they anticipate a fall in the market rate, then bonds are preferred because of the capital gain which their price rise implies.

At relatively high rates of interest, people will be more likely to predict a fall, and therefore the demand for 'speculative' or 'idle' money balances (*Mdi*) will be lower.

Keynes also believed that there was a minimum rate of interest within this theory of liquidity preference. This arises for two reasons. First, there will come a point at which everybody agrees that interest rates can only rise; bond transactions cease. Second, the costs involved in buying and selling bonds outweigh any perceived capital gains; bond prices are already so high that any further rise which might occur would tend to be very small. This then produces a relationship as shown in Figure 4.2.

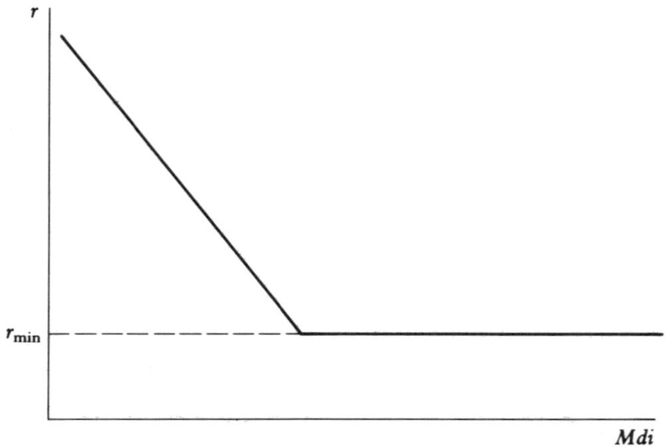

Figure 4.2 *The demand for idle money balances*

This theory was modified in 1958 by an American economist, James Tobin, who substantiated a fourth demand for money, the *asset* demand. This again refers to the role of money in portfolios of assets, but stresses the role of bond holdings as a source of income through their yield rather than any capital gain which they may provide. It is introduced here in part to avoid a common misinterpretation of Keynes' 'speculative' motive. The asset demand explains that people hold less money when interest rates are high because the opportunity cost of holding it is high. Under the speculative demand this occurs because people predict that a fall in the rate of interest is more likely than a rise, so they wish to hold a higher proportion of bonds as bond prices are predicted to rise and a capital gain can be made.

If the speculative and asset demands are incorporated in one overall demand for 'idle' balances, then the total demand for money under the Keynesian system can be expressed as:

$$Md = Mda + Mdi$$

where Md = demand for real money balances
Mda = demand for active money
Mdi = demand for idle money

The determination of the equilibrium rate of interest

For any given level of income the total demand for money is equated to the money supply through changes in the speculative demand due to changes in the rate of interest. These are changes in the 'real' money supply which is a measure of the *effective* supply of money, when changes in the average price level have been allowed for. Given the simplifying assumptions made above, each level of income implies a specific and unique demand for active balances. If the money supply changes, then it is through changes in the demand for idle balances that the total demand for money must adjust. These, as indicated above, are related to the rate of interest. Consider the economy where:

$$\text{income} = Y_0$$
$$\text{real money supply} = MS_0.$$

Of the fixed money supply, Mda_0 is demanded for active balances. For equilibrium in the money market Mdi_0 must be demanded for idle balances, giving an equilibrium rate of interest r_0. If the money supply were to increase for the same level of income Y_0 then individuals would find that their holdings of money as opposed to bonds were too high; they would demand more bonds, thus raising bond prices and, in effect, reducing the rate of interest.

The notion of a minimum rate of interest implies that, beyond a certain point, increases in the money supply will not lead to further

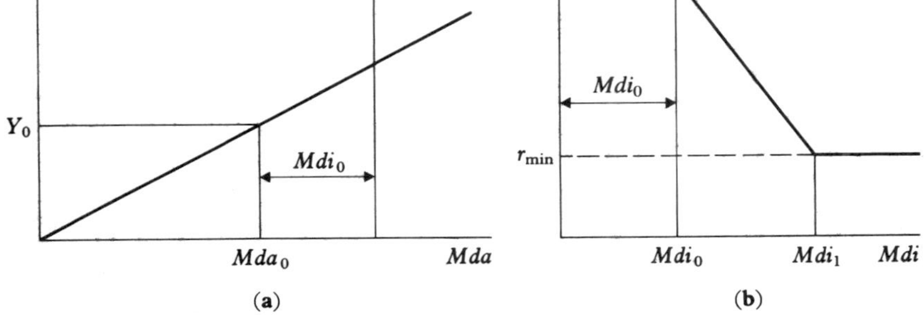

Figure 4.3 *The equilibrium rate of interest*

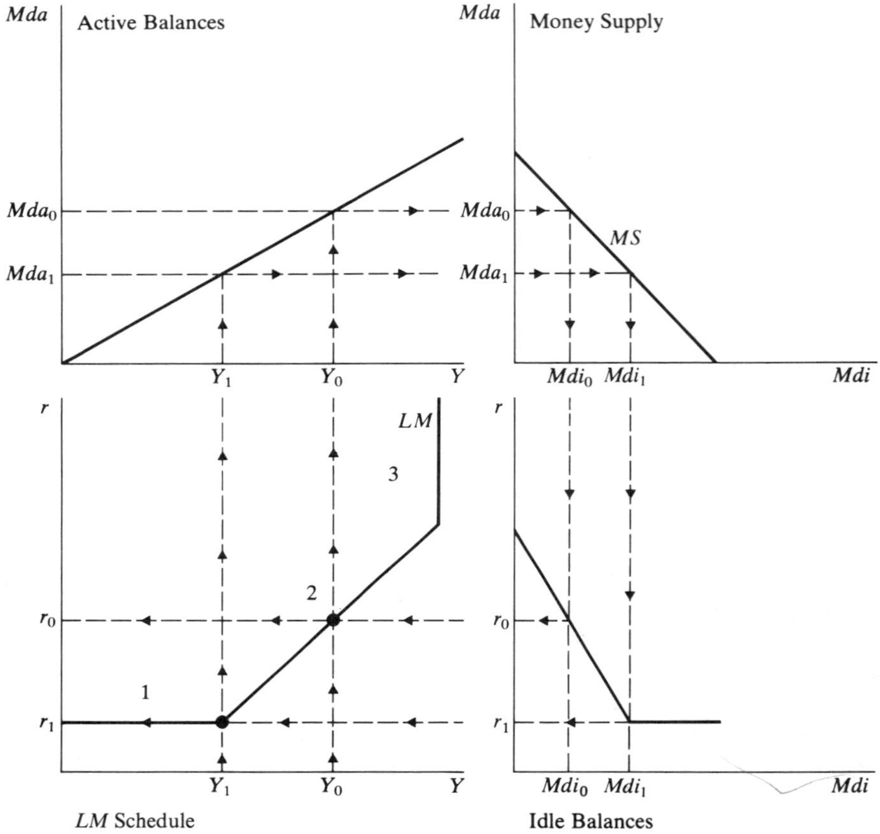

Figure 4.4 *The derivation of the* LM *schedule*

reductions in the rate for any given level of income. Increases in the money supply lead to a simple expansion of idle balances. This corresponds to the horizontal area of the liquidity preference schedule from Mdi_1 onwards.

The *LM* schedule

From the above analysis it is possible to map out various income levels and rates of interest which correspond to equilibrium in the money market for a particular level of real money supply.

In Figure 4.4 the total demand for active and idle balances, $Mda + Mdi$, must equal the fixed money supply MS. Starting at income Y_0 the demand for active balances will be Mda_0 leaving Mdi_0 of the money supply held in idle balances; this produces an interest rate of r_0. Y_0r_0 is therefore an equilibrium condition on the *LM* schedule. If income were to fall to Y_1, the demand for active balances would fall to Mda_1 causing an increase in idle balances to Mdi_1 and a lower rate of interest r_1. Thus Y_1r_1 also lies on the *LM* schedule. If income were to fall below Y_1 the demand for active balances would fall; the increase in idle balances which results no longer affects the rate of interest since it occurs on the horizontal section of the idle balance schedule. The equilibrium rate of interest is constant at r_1 for income levels below Y_1. At the opposite extreme, the level of income is constrained by the size of the money supply; it cannot exceed the point at which the whole money supply is required for active balances.

The *LM* schedule therefore demonstrates how the interest rate adjusts to equate the demand for and supply of money at different levels of income. In theory its shape will include the following main characteristics, illustrated in Figure 4.4.

Range 1 refers to the liquidity trap, the full implications of which will be considered in Chapter 5.

Range 2 refers to the intermediate stage where, given a fixed money supply, higher levels of income call forth greater demands for active money, a lower demand for idle money, and hence higher rates of interest.

Range 3 refers to the level of income where all the money supply is required for active purposes. This corresponds to the Classical view that money is only demanded as a means of exchange.

The *LM* schedule will shift in response to a change in the 'real' money supply. It will therefore change position if the nominal money supply changes, in the absence of any change in the average price level, or if the price level changes but the nominal money supply remains constant. An increase in the real money supply will shift the *LM* schedule outwards to the right. At any given level of income, and hence demand for active balances, any increase in the real money supply must be held as increased idle balances and so reduces the rate of interest. Each level of income is associated with a lower rate of interest. A fall in the real money supply will have the opposite effect. At each level of income idle balances are reduced so forcing up the rate of interest. The *LM* schedule shifts back to the left.

Additional reading

In addition to modern texts on the subject the reader may wish to look at:

1. Kaldor, N. and Trevithick, J. 'A Keynesian Perspective on Money', *Lloyds Bank Review*, 1981.
2. Laidler, D. (1977) *The Demand for Money: Theories and Evidence*, 2nd edn, Dun-Donelley.
3. Ritter, L. S. 'The Rôle of Money in Keynesian Theory' in M. G. Mueller, *Readings in Macroeconomics*, 2nd edn, Holt International, 1971.
4. Tobin, J. 'Liquidity Preference as Behaviour towards Risk' in M. G. Mueller, *Readings in Macroeconomics*, 2nd edn, Holt International, 1971.

5.

The *IS–LM* model

Having illustrated and explained how the *IS* and *LM* schedules can be derived, and having considered the determinants of their respective slopes and positions, it is appropriate to combine them in the *IS–LM* model. As in the preceding analysis of their derivation, it will be assumed for the purposes of simplicity and clarity that each schedule arises from a set of linear relationships. For the same reasons this assumption is extended in later sections to restrict analysis to the intermediate range of the *LM* schedule. While straight lines may aid exposition, it is not claimed that curved lines would be unlikely to occur if the schedules could actually be observed in practice.

The *IS–LM* model in the closed economy

The two schedules are combined to yield a rate of interest and level of income which correspond to equilibrium in both the 'real' or goods and services sector and the monetary sector. This is illustrated in Figure 5.1.

Shifts in either curve will create a new equilibrium level of income and rate of interest. In policy terms the *IS* curve is shifted through fiscal measures and the *LM* curve through monetary measures. The relative effectiveness of each policy option is determined by the relative slopes of the curves as the following analysis illustrates.

Consider the case of fiscal policy. If, for example, government expenditure is raised, all other things being equal, income would be expected to rise through the multiplier process. The extent to which this occurs in the model depends upon the amount by which interest rates also rise (see Figure 5.2).

In the liquidity trap the increase in government expenditure shifts the *IS* schedule from IS_0 to IS_1 causing income to rise from Y_0 to Y_1. This represents the full multiplier effect which the 'Keynesian Cross' diagram in Figure 5.3 indicates.

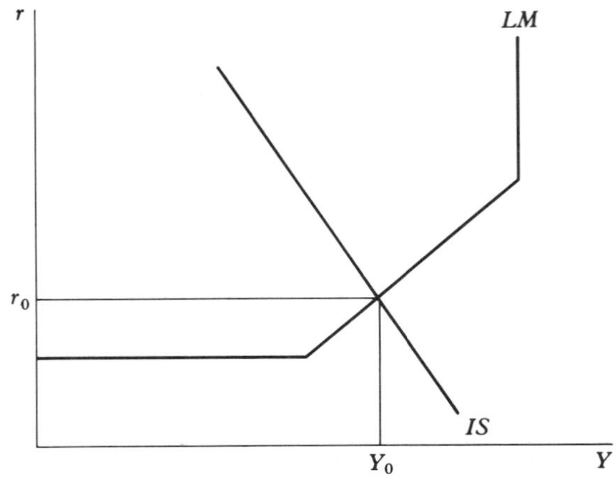

Figure 5.1 *The* IS–LM *equilibrium*

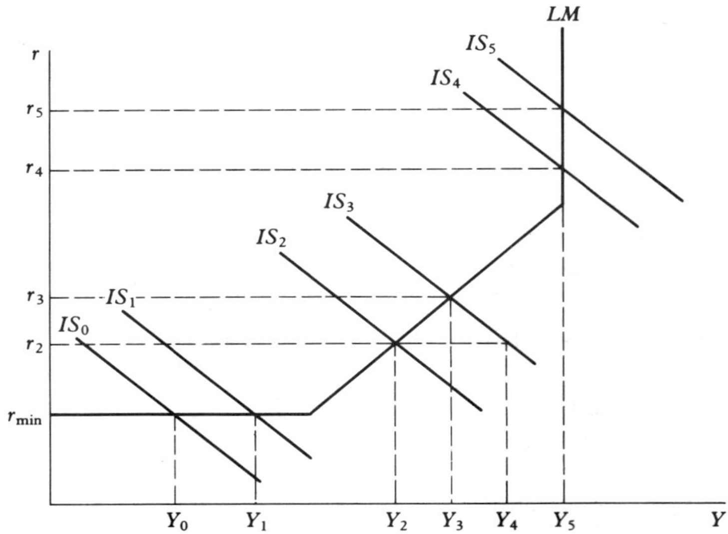

Figure 5.2 *Fiscal policy and the slope of the* LM *schedule*

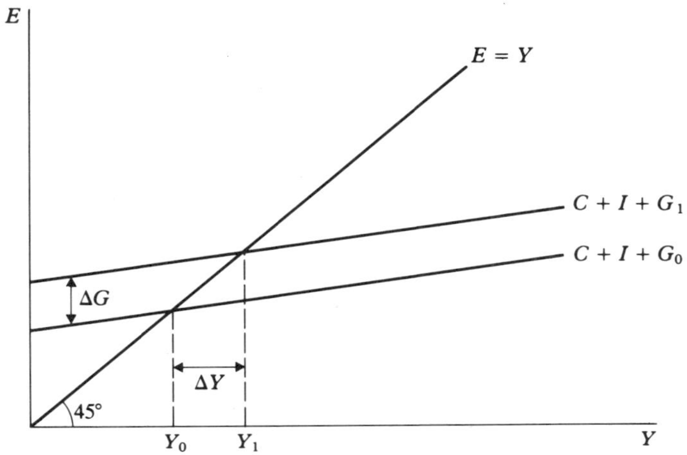

Figure 5.3 *Equilibrium income and the 'Keynesian Cross': The full multiplier effect*

Fiscal policy is most effective in the particular case of the liquidity trap where the *LM* schedule is flat (see Figure 5.2), because idle money balances are reduced without affecting the price of bonds and hence the rate of interest.

In the intermediate range where the *LM* schedule is upward sloping, a rightward shift of the *IS* schedule from IS_2 to IS_3 only raises income to Y_3 and not Y_4. Part of the rise in income is counteracted by a fall in investment due to the higher interest rate. The rate of interest rises from r_2 to r_3 as people reduce idle money balances in order to enable the higher level of active transactions required to support the higher level of income. In this case fiscal policy is only partially effective since part of the effect of increasing government expenditure is to crowd out some private investment (see Figure 5.4).

In the final range the entire multiplier effect is offset by the reduction in investment as interest rates rise. The whole money supply is used for active purposes and income is constrained to the level Y_5.

The *LM* schedule shifts in response to a change in the 'real' money supply. A reduction will shift the *LM* curve to the left because a larger proportion is required for active purposes and idle balances fall. The opposite occurs in the event of an increase (see Figure 5.5).

In the liquidity trap monetary policy is ineffective because the increase in money supply is simply used to expand idle balances without increasing bond transactions. The rate of interest remains unaltered

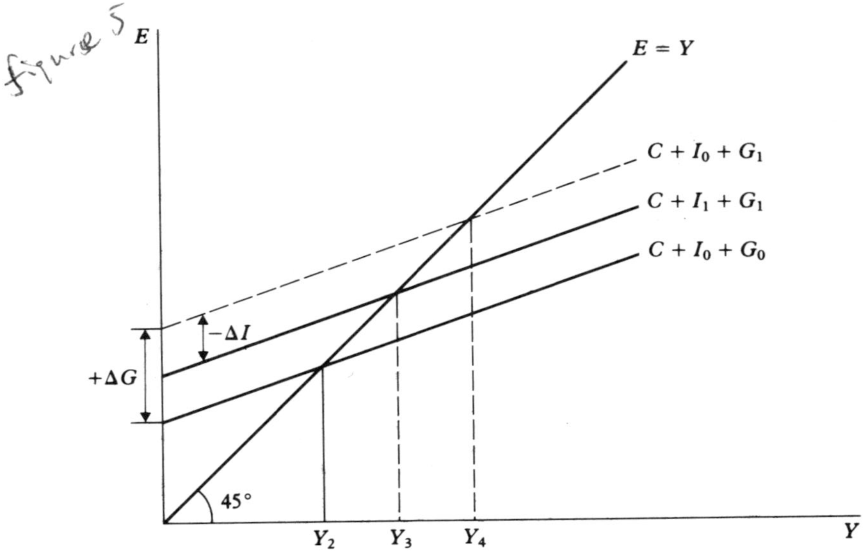

Figure 5.4 *Equilibrium income and the 'Keynesian Cross': The case of partial crowding out*

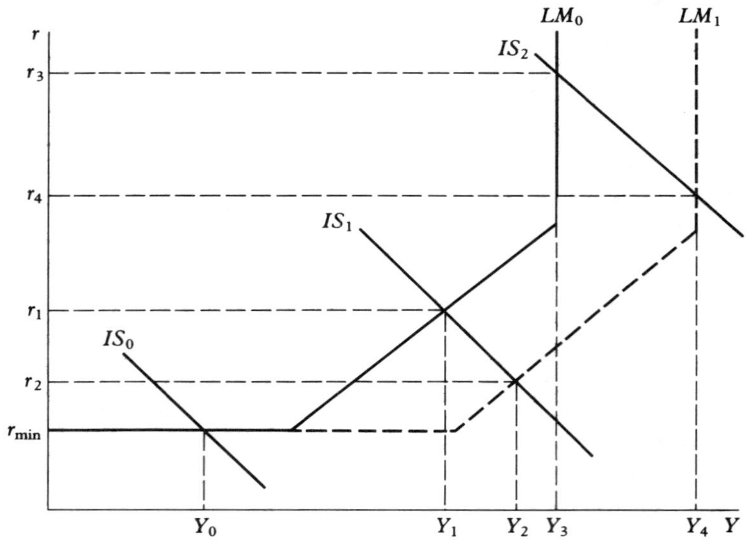

Figure 5.5 *Monetary policy and the* LM *schedule*

and therefore so does investment. In the intermediate range income increases due to the fall in interest rates and the rise in investment which that causes. Part of the fall in interest rates is offset by the upward pressure which arises from the increase in demand for active balances as incomes rise. In the final range this does not occur because all money is used for active purposes; the increase in its supply is fully transmitted in terms of the increase in economic activity which it enables.

In the case of a shift in the *LM* schedule, the effects upon income and interest will, to some extent, be determined by the slope of the *IS* schedule.

In the liquidity trap, part (a) of Figure 5.6, the slope of the *IS* schedule does not affect either income or the rate of interest. Increases in the money supply are accumulated as idle balances.

In the intermediate range it affects both. The steeper or more interest-inelastic the *IS* schedule, the less income responds to a shift in *LM* and the more interest rates change. Income responds less either because investment is relatively interest-insensitive, or because the multiplier is small, or both. As a result, a larger proportion of the increase in the money supply is added to idle balances since it is not required for active purposes; the fall in the rate of interest is larger. In the case of IS_1 investment sensitivity and/or the multiplier are greater, inducing a greater increase in real income, a larger rise in the demand for active balances and hence a smaller drop in the rate of interest.

In the final range only interest rates are affected by variations in the slope of the *IS* schedule.

In its simple form, as described above, the *IS–LM* model indicates how government can affect income and the rate of interest through fiscal or monetary policy. By changing government expenditure and/or taxation they shift the *IS* schedule; by changing the money supply they shift the *LM* schedule. The relative effectiveness of either is determined by the relative slopes of the two schedules.

In the context of the *IS–LM* framework Keynesians believe that the *IS* schedule is steep and investment is relatively insensitive to changes in the rate of interest and that the *LM* schedule is shallow and interest rates are insensitive to changes in the money supply. From this it is clear that Keynesians will tend to stress fiscal policy as a means of affecting the level of economic activity; changes in taxation and/or government expenditure will be more effective than changes in the money supply.

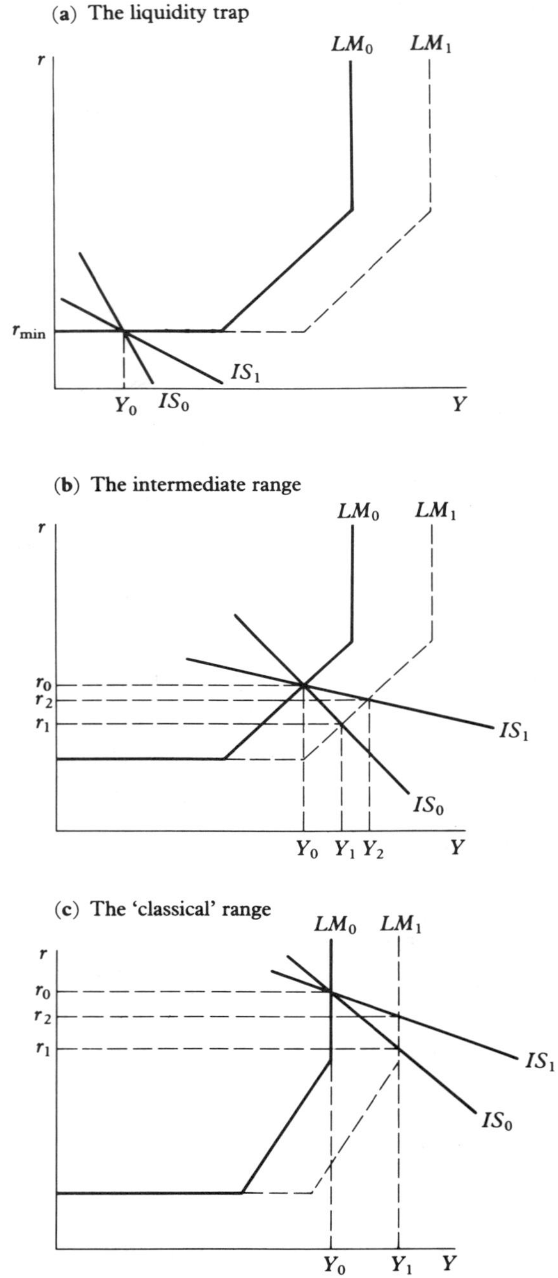

Figure 5.6 *Monetary policy with differently sloped* IS *schedules*

It is important to recognize, however, that fiscal and monetary policies are interrelated; shifts in one schedule may also move the other. For example, if the *IS* schedule shifts to the right as a result of an increase in government expenditure which is financed by creating money or credit, then the money supply may rise and the *LM* schedule also shifts to the right.

The *IS–LM* model in the open economy

Up to this point the treatment of the determination of equilibrium income has been confined to the closed economy. However, as indicated in Chapter 2, the balance of trade forms an important element in the economy's aggregate demand. It now remains to indicate the implications of including the trade balance and the overall balance of payments in the *IS–LM* framework. What follows is of necessity a simplified view of the world. The complexities of the foreign exchange markets, and in particular the role of expectations and speculation, make the whole area very difficult to model realistically. The main simplifying assumption that is made here is of *perfect capital markets.*

The capital market in this instance refers to the movement of monies between countries to enable purchases of assets or bonds. In general such money will move to the country which offers the greatest return in the form of interest. The assumption of perfect capital markets, or perfect mobility of capital, implies that any real interest rate differential will generate a movement of financial assets into the country which has the higher rate of return, that movement continuing until such time as the differential is removed. In practice, of course, nominal interest rates are not identical across all countries, because they include some allowance for inflation and the expected depreciation/appreciation of the country's currency relative to those of her major trading partners.

In addition to assuming that capital flows are related to relative interest rates, it is necessary to specify the determinants of imports and exports. As indicated in Chapter 2, import demand is related to the level of domestic income, the domestic price level and the exchange rate, while export demand is determined by the domestic price level and the exchange rate.

THE FOREIGN EXCHANGE MARKET

The value of a country's currency in terms of the amount of another country's currency that it can purchase is known as the exchange rate. To simplify the explanation, imagine a situation where there are only two currencies, pounds sterling and American dollars. All goods purchased in Britain must be paid for in pounds, whilst all American goods must be purchased in dollars. The demand for pounds is thus a reflection of the desire of American individuals and firms to convert dollars into pounds so as to purchase British goods, services and financial assets. The supply of pounds is a reflection of the desire by British individuals and firms to convert pounds into dollars so as to purchase American goods, services and financial assets.

When the price of one currency in terms of another increases, it is said to *appreciate*, and likewise when its value falls it *depreciates*. If the pound/dollar exchange rate depreciated from \$4/£ to \$2/£, the dollar price of British goods falls, since a good costing £1 now only costs \$2 rather than \$4. Thus, other things being equal, as the pound depreciates, British goods become cheaper and more pounds are demanded. Provided that UK prices remain unaltered, export revenue must rise because more goods and services are being demanded at the given UK price level. Similarly if the pound were to appreciate from \$2/£ to \$4/£, the price of American goods and services becomes relatively cheaper to UK residents and the desire to convert pounds into dollars increases. The supply of pounds is greater the more dollars there are to the pound. The equilibrium exchange rate will be that at which the demand for pounds is just equal to the supply as shown in Figure 5.7.

Given the reasoning above, the demand schedule D_0 must slope down from left to right, while the supply curve S_0 slopes upwards from left to right. The equilibrium exchange rate is E_0 at which Q_0 £s are traded.

If there is an increased desire on the part of Americans to purchase British goods, at any given exchange rate, the demand curve will shift out to the right D_1 and the exchange rate will appreciate to E_1. For a given supply an increased demand will be met by bidding up the price. It follows that an increased supply of pounds to the market will cause a depreciation in the pound's value against the dollar.

There are three ways in which the exchange rate may be determined. First, as indicated above, by the interaction of the forces of demand and supply. Thus the increase in demand to D_1 resulted in a higher exchange rate. These are known as flexible or free-floating exchange rates. Second, the monetary authorities may set a predetermined rate

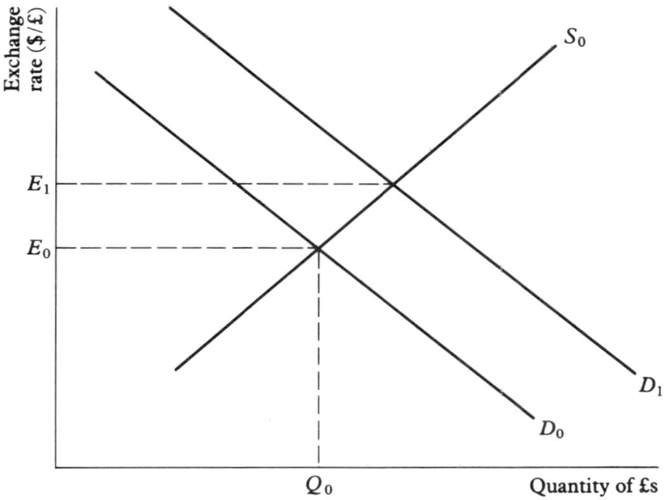

Figure 5.7 *The determination of the equilibrium exchange rate*

of exchange, known as a fixed exchange rate. The third involves some combination of the two.

The principles of fixed exchange rates are illustrated in Figure 5.8. Suppose that the authorities have set the exchange rate at E_0 and that

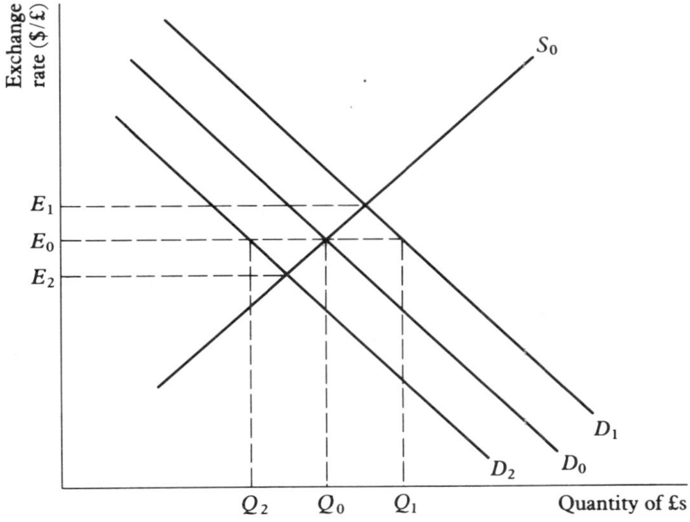

Figure 5.8 *The foreign exchange market with a fixed exchange rate*

this is the initial equilibrium position. There then follows an increase in the demand for pounds D_1. Under floating exchange rates this would cause the pound to appreciate to E_1, but the rate is held at E_0. At E_0 there is an excess demand for pounds over the supply $(Q_1 - Q_0)$. If upward pressure on the pound is to be averted, more pounds must be made available. It is the central monetary authority which makes pounds available at a price E_0, supplying $Q_1 - Q_0$. This has two results. First, the pounds are exchanged for dollars. These dollars are held by the authority and its holdings of foreign currency increase. This is known as the foreign exchange reserve. Second, the pounds supplied $Q_1 - Q_0$ are spent by Americans on UK goods and services and thus enter the domestic flow of economic activity. Since the authorities have had to release $Q_1 - Q_0$ extra pounds, it follows that the UK's money supply will have increased by exactly $Q_1 - Q_0$. This can only be prevented if the authorities sell government bonds for pounds to domestic residents, thus withdrawing the money from circulation. This is a process known as sterilization.

A fall in the demand for £s to D_2 creates an excess supply at exchange rate E_0 of $Q_0 - Q_2$. In this case to prevent a fall in the value of the pound the authorities must purchase $Q_0 - Q_2$ pounds in the market. These pounds must be paid for in terms of dollars and thus the foreign exchange reserves are reduced and the domestic money supply is reduced by $Q_0 - Q_2$. A process of sterilization, but now purchasing bonds for pounds, could negate the monetary effects of the balance of payments deficit.

From the above discussion it follows that when operating under a fixed exchange rate regime, a country's monetary policy will be influenced by the supply and demand for its currency. In the UK an excess demand for pounds, a balance of payments surplus, will cause an expansion of the money supply and hence a rightward shift in the *LM* schedule. Conversely, an excess supply and a balance of payments deficit will cause the *LM* schedule to shift to the left as the money supply contracts.

A further implication of fixed exchange rates is currency value misalignment. This occurs when a country's currency is perpetually subject to either excess demand or excess supply, producing continued balance of payments surpluses or deficits. This was the experience of West Germany and the UK respectively in the late 1960s and 1970s.

Eventually a devaluation or revaluation has to take place to bring the exchange rate closer to its true equilibrium value. In either case such movements may be hastened by the role of foreign exchange speculators. For example if a devaluation of the pound is rumoured, speculators holding pounds or UK-based financial assets will attempt to exchange these for alternative currencies, increasing the supply of pounds to the market and creating a greater excess supply at the fixed rate. This may place an intolerable burden on the foreign exchange reserve and a devaluation becomes inevitable. This is the classic 'run on the pound'.

The last form of exchange rate regime is the 'dirty float'. This refers to a situation where currencies are allowed to find a long-run equilibrium value but where the monetary authorities are prepared to intervene in the short run to damp down any rapid shifts in the supply and demand schedules. Thus if the currency was depreciating, the domestic authorities may enter the market to purchase pounds so as to smooth out the downward pressure rather than to offer any long-term support.

Fiscal and monetary policy with fixed exchange rates

The assumption of perfect capital markets implies that the real rate of interest across countries will be the same. Suppose that this rate is associated with real income Y_0 in the country defined by IS_0 and LM_0 in Figure 5.9.

As in the closed economy, a fiscal expansion shifts the IS curve out to the right, for example to IS_1. This raises the level of income but also raises the domestic interest rate to r_1, given the fixed money supply. The higher interest rate in turn attracts an inflow capital, which causes an excess demand in the currency market. There is a balance of payments surplus. As we have already seen, unless the authorities take preventive action this leads back to an expansion of the domestic money supply. Since an equilibrium cannot be re-established until the interest rate differential is eliminated, the money supply must continue to expand until the LM schedule intersects IS_1 at r_w. The new level of income is Y_1 and the fiscal expansion has been fully effective. There has been no increase in the rate of interest as is generally the case in the closed economy model. Similar effects would result from an exogenous increase in exports. A deflationary fiscal policy would produce a fully multiplied fall in income.

A monetary expansion may be represented by a shift in the LM schedule from LM_0 to LM_1. With IS_0 this produces a fall in the rate of interest and higher income, because of the resultant influence on

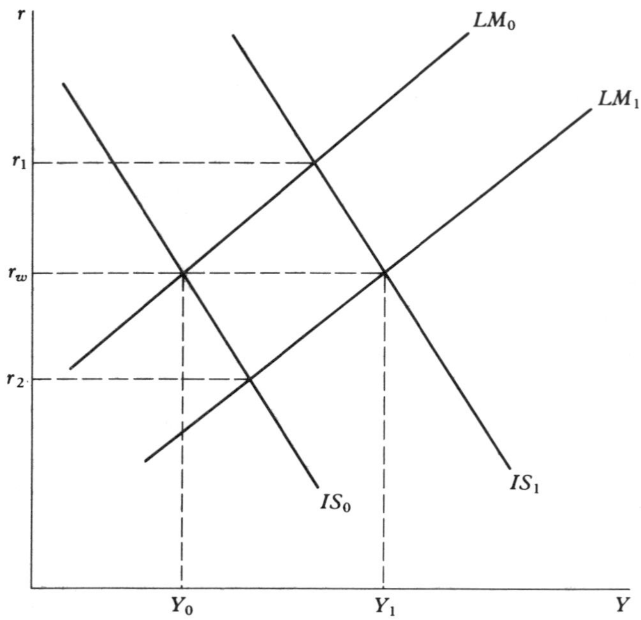

Figure 5.9 *Fiscal and monetary policies under fixed and flexible exchange rates*

investment expenditures. However, the lower interest rate must cause capital to flow out of the country, creating excess supply in the currency market and reducing the money supply. As in the fiscal case, this adjustment continues until the interest rate differential is removed, such that LM shifts back to LM_0 to give r_w. The monetary expansion will have reduced the level of foreign exchange reserve but will have had no effect on income.

A third policy option with fixed exchange rates is devaluation. Recall that aggregate demand may be written as

$$Y = C + I + G + (X - M)$$

The items $C + I + G$ are often referred to as the level of domestic absorption A which gives

$$Y = A + (X - M)$$

A government may attempt to remedy a persistent balance of trade deficit by devaluing its currency. In short this makes exports cheaper in the overseas markets and hence more attractive, and imports more expensive and so less attractive. $(X - M)$ increases and the IS curve will shift to the right. This in turn produces a higher level of income. Since both C and I are expected to be positively related to Y, the level of domestic absorption will also increase. Further, the higher level of income also raises import demand. Thus, if the balance of trade is to be improved, some form of fiscal deflation is necessary to prevent A from rising. It seems most unlikely that a devaluation, by itself, will have any long-term influence on the balance of trade or the balance of payments.

Fiscal and monetary policies with flexible exchange rates

The major difference between the flexible and fixed rate analysis is that, under a flexible rate, excess demand or supply for the currency is removed by exchange rate movements, not by the monetary authorities buying and selling in the market. There is therefore no reason to suppose that a domestic fiscal or monetary policy will have any secondary monetary effects, but because the exchange rate adjusts it will influence the value of exports and imports.

A fiscal expansion will, as before, shift the IS curve to IS_1, raising income and the rate of interest above r_w. Demand for the domestic currency increases with the advent of the capital inflow. The demand curve shifts out, as in Figure 5.7, causing the exchange rate to appreciate. At a higher exchange rate with a given set of domestic and world prices, imports become relatively cheaper and exports relatively more expensive. This implies that the trade balance must worsen, $X - M$ becomes smaller, and the IS curve shifts back to IS_0 to remove the interest rate differential. The expansionary effects are exactly offset by the deterioration in the balance of trade. Note however that the countries supplying imports are now better off. Their exports have been increased, and the fiscal expansion is in effect 'exported' to these countries.

A fiscal contraction would also have no effect on income, but would be offset by an improvement in the balance of trade.

A monetary expansion moves the LM curve to LM_1 lowering the rate of interest and raising income. The resultant outflow of capital increases the supply of domestic currency and the exchange rate depreciates. The reverse of the fiscal expansion is true. The trade balance improves as imports become more expensive and exports cheaper; the IS curve will also shift out to the right. In Figure 5.9 this would be to IS_1 where r_w is again the real market rate of interest. The monetary expansion has a fully multiplied effect on domestic income, by way of the trade balance. It follows that there must have been a corresponding income reduction abroad, because overseas exports have fallen and imports increased.

POLICY CONCLUSIONS FROM THE *IS–LM* MODEL

The policy conclusions derived from the simple *IS–LM* framework may be over-simplistic. First, the possible effects of a change in income level upon the domestic price level and the subsequent repercussions this may have for wage levels, inflation and unemployment have been ignored. This is the subject matter of Chapter 6.

Second, in the open economy model, policy conclusions are reached by ignoring the effects of domestic policy actions on foreign economies. For example, under a flexible exchange rate regime it is unlikely that a country will allow another to export its unemployment by means of an expansionary domestic monetary policy. Some retaliation is to be expected. This would prevent the *IS* shift and produce an overall effect much the same as in the closed model.

Third, fiscal and monetary policies have been considered in isolation. It is rare that governments pursue a single policy. Thus, if Y_1 in Figure 5.9 were the objective, this could be brought about by a combined fiscal and monetary expansion, moving IS_0 to IS_1 and LM_0 to LM_1, with no disruptive effects on the foreign exchange market.

Additional reading

Most of the material in this chapter can be found in any good modern macroeconomics text. In addition see:

1. Metcalfe, J. S. 'Foreign Trade and the Balance of Payments' in A. R. Prest and D. J. Coppock (eds.), *The U.K. Economy: Manual of Applied Economics*, Weidenfeld and Nicolson, 1982. (A commentary on recent UK exchange rate and balance of payment policies.)
2. Samuelson, P. A. 'The Simple Mathematics of Income Determination' in M. G. Mueller, *Readings in Macroeconomics*, 2nd edn, Holt International, 1971. (Some knowledge of calculus required.)

6.

Output, prices and employment

The preceding chapters have given an account of the traditional Keynesian model as depicted in the *IS–LM* framework. Where appropriate, this has been contrasted with the Classical model of the macroeconomy to reveal distinct differences in the assumptions and predictions of each.

Throughout this discussion little or no reference has been made to the determination of the price level and the level of unemployment. A given level of income will, in the short run, correspond to a certain level of employment, but so far the analysis has precluded any consideration of the extent and nature of any associated unemployment.

The *IS–LM* framework determines the equilibrium income and interest rate. It is implicit that different levels of income may be achieved through fiscal and monetary changes with minimal attention to the price level.

The events of the late 1960s onward cast severe doubts on the applicability of this model. As in the 1930s new problems led to the development of new theories of the macroeconomy. Keynesians had to consider in more detail the determination of the price level, and two new developments of classical macroeconomics also arose: the Modern Monetarists and the New Classical school.

The fundamentals of the debate have centred on the very core of macroeconomics—the extent to which government is able, by means of *aggregate demand management*, to bring about favourable economic change. The Keynesians believe that such intervention is both beneficial and necessary in certain circumstances, but have been forced to concede that prolonged fiscal or monetary expansion will generally result in inflation. Both the Modern Monetarist and New Classical schools have questioned the ability of the government to have any lasting influence on macroeconomic policy goals.

These differing conclusions depend on the view taken of three crucial areas of the macroeconomy. These are:

1. The speed with which markets adjust to a new, or the original, equilibrium following some disturbance.
2. The subjective trade-off between the short-run gains of a policy and its possible long-run consequences.
3. The way in which individuals form expectations of future economic events such as the future levels of prices and wages.

A convenient means of addressing these debates is by way of the aggregate demand and supply schedules for the economy.

The aggregate demand schedule

The *aggregate demand schedule* (*ADS*) is a relationship between the price level and the level of real income, the amount of goods and services produced. The price level is the average price of all the goods and services produced in the economy. The *ADS* then shows the different combinations of the price level and real income at which planned spending and output are equal.

A simple way of deriving the *ADS* is from the *IS–LM* framework. To achieve this it is necessary to ask the hypothetical question 'What happens to the *IS–LM* equilibrium as the price level changes?' Since the *LM* function is drawn for a given real money supply, movements in the price level affect the real money supply and hence cause the *LM* function to shift (see Chapter 4). Similarly if changes in the price level cause individuals to perceive a change in their wealth and hence adjust their consumption, then the level of real demand will be altered and the *IS* curve will shift.

Assuming for simplicity that only the *LM* function is influenced by the price level, then the *ADS* may be derived as shown in Figure 6.1.

Let the initial conditions be LM_0 (P_0) and IS_0 with a price level of P_0. Real and money market equilibrium produces a level of income of Y_0, hence the combination P_0, Y_0 is a point on the ADS_0. If the price level were to fall to P_1, with a given nominal money supply, the real money supply would increase, shifting *LM* to the right from LM_0 (P_0) to $LM_1(P_1)$. The interest rate falls, producing higher investment and hence the higher level of income Y_1. $P_1 Y_1$ is therefore on the *ADS* which slopes downwards from left to right, because a lower price level induces a higher real money supply, a lower interest rate and hence a

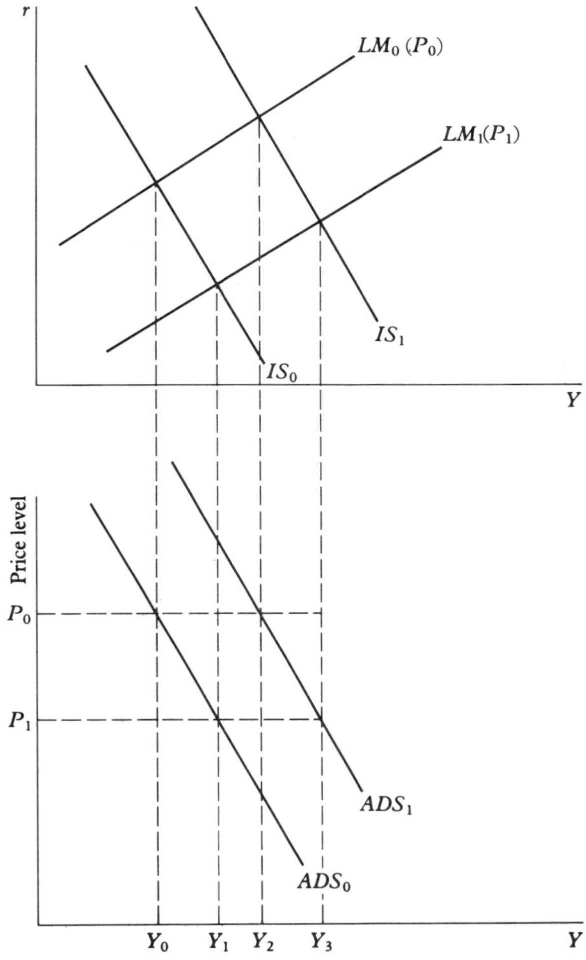

Figure 6.1 *The aggregate demand schedule*

higher equilibrium income. It is important to note that, since the *ADS* is derived from the *IS–LM* framework which shows real and monetary equilibrium, each price/income combination on the *ADS* also implies an equilibrium rate of interest.

It is clear from Figure 6.1 that the *ADS* can be 'mapped out' by movements of the *LM* schedule along the *IS* schedule. It follows therefore that shifts in the *IS* schedule will also shift the *ADS* in a similar direction. This is illustrated by IS_1 and ADS_1 in the diagram.

Aggregate supply—The Classical case

The *aggregate supply schedule* depicts the amount of output an economy is willing to produce at each fixed price level. It is derived by considering the labour market and the short-run aggregate production function. The short-run production function is based on the assumption of a given quantity of capital stock. Output is then varied by employing more labour to work with that capital. The higher the level of employment, the greater the output, although the contribution of each additional worker is expected to decline as the capital is used more intensively.

As was discussed in Chapter 1, the Classical model assumes freely adjusting markets through the price mechanism. This applies to all markets including the labour market.

The labour market represents the supply of and demand for labour. In the Classical model both the quantity of labour demanded by employers and that supplied by the work force are determined by the real wages. (The real wage rate is the money wage divided by the price level.) Given price flexibility, there are good theoretical grounds why this should be the case. Rational producers will employ labour up to the point where the cost of employing the last or marginal worker is just equal to the value of his/her output or marginal product. If the price level falls, all other things being equal, real wages will rise and the value of the marginal product will fall. The same real quantity of goods and services are valued at the lower price level. Thus, in aggregate, the demand for labour will fall as the real wage rises. Like the *ADS*, the labour demand schedule slopes *down* from left to right.

The supply-of-labour schedule will slope *upwards* from left to right. The willingness to work increases as the real wage rate rises. As the reward for work, or compensation for loss of leisure, gets greater, so more people are prepared to enter the work force.

The labour market equilibrium is shown in Figure 6.2. The equilibrium level of employment is N_0 at real wage W_0/P_0, where W_0 = the initial money wage and P_0 = the price level. Since supply is equal to demand there is no involuntary unemployment. N_0 may be referred to as the natural or 'full' level of employment. This does not of course mean that all workers have jobs; rather, it implies that all those willing to work for wage W_0/P_0 will be employed. Those unable or unwilling to work will remain unemployed; the logic of the model implies that this is a voluntary decision.

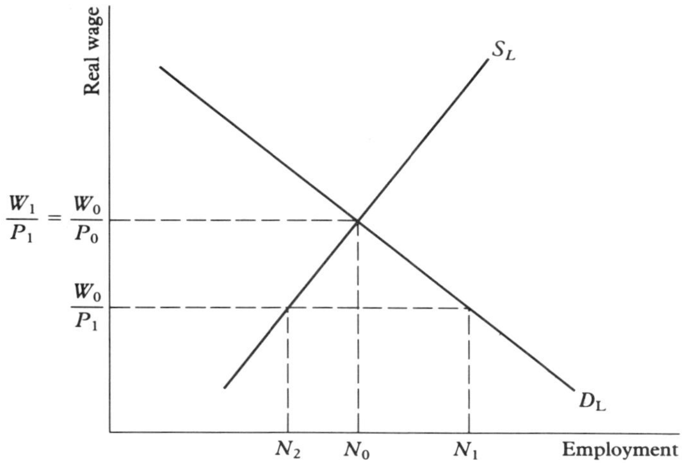

Figure 6.2 *The classical labour market equilibrium*

The equilibrium will be disrupted by a change in either the price or the wage level. Consider an increase in the price level. This lowers the real wage to, say, W_0/P_1. The demand for employment rises to N_1, while supply falls to N_2; then there is excess demand in the market. Given that wages are *flexible* and adjust *quickly*, the excess demand will cause an increase in the money wage rate until the market is again in equilibrium at N_0 with real wage W_1/P_1, where $W_1/P_1 = W_0/P_0$; prices and money wages have simply risen by the same amount

If an economy has a given quantity of capital with which to employ labour, it follows from the above analysis that the level of supply does not change given different price levels. The aggregate supply schedule (*ASS*), showing the amount of output an economy will produce at each fixed price level, is vertical (Figure 6.3).

CLASSICAL POLICY IMPLICATIONS

The equilibrium price level and real income is given by the intersection of *ADS* and *ASS* in Figure 6.4.

The policy implications of Figure 6.4 are profound. Consider the case of a monetary expansion. The lower interest rates which this would induce raise aggregate demand to ADS_1, but this has no effect on the level of real income Y_0. At price level P_0 and ADS_1 there would be excess demand for goods and labour; prices are rapidly bid up to restore equilibrium at P_1. Monetary policy is said to be neutral since it

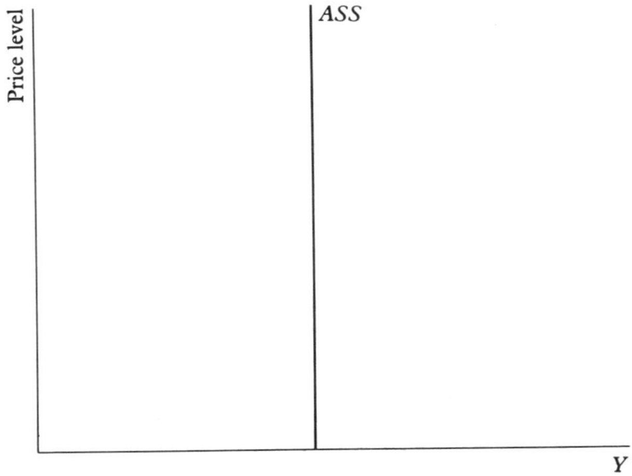

Figure 6.3 *The classical aggregate supply schedule*

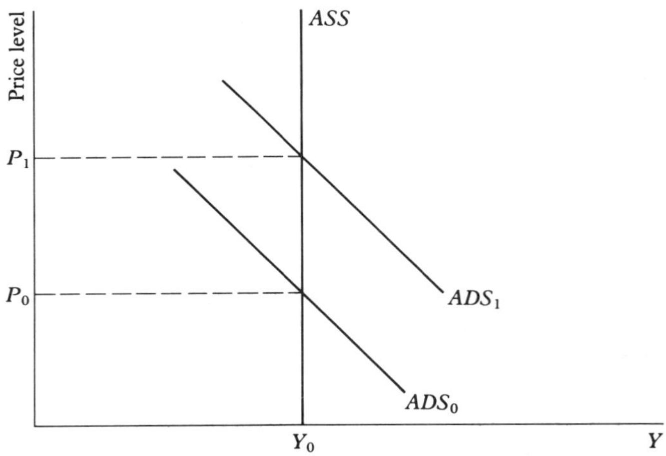

Figure 6.4 *Determination of the price level: The classical case*

only influences nominal values through the price level. It is possible to be more specific: since real values remain unaltered, a given percentage increase in the nominal money supply must induce an identical rise in prices.

In the event of a dynamic monetary expansion, e.g., an annual growth of the money supply by 10 per cent, a continuing increase in the price level of 10 per cent per annum would result.

Aggregate supply—The Keynesian case

Central to the Classical view of the *ASS* is the flexibility of money wages and hence real wages. The fundamental difference between the Classical and Keynesian *ASS*s rests on the treatment of wage flexibility in the labour market. Keynes introduced the assumption of wage rate rigidity. In particular he assumed that money wages would be flexible in an upward direction but, because of imperfections in the labour market, downward movements in the money wage would be very difficult to achieve. The implication of this is that, while an excess demand for labour would be only short-lived because the money wage would be quickly bid up, an excess supply would persist as money wages would not be equally quickly bid down. The labour market is in disequilibrium with involuntary or 'Keynesian' unemployment. This situation is depicted in Figure 6.5.

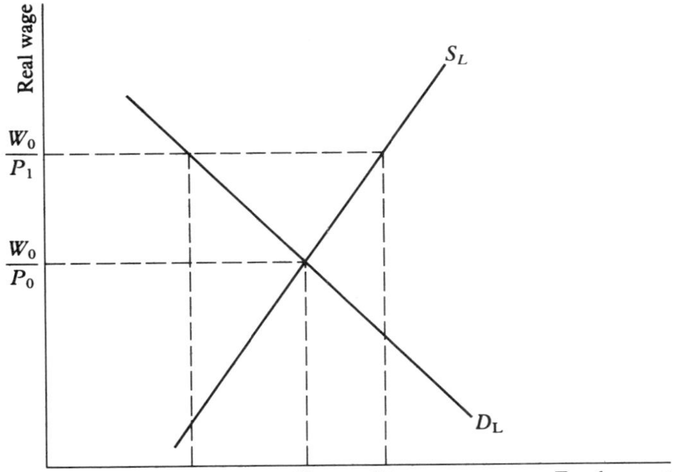

Figure 6.5 *The Keynesian labour market equilibrium*

The market-clearing position is given by real wage W_0/P_0 and level of employment N_0. A rise in the price level would reduce real wages and create an excess demand for labour. Since the money wage is still upwardly flexible, this excess demand cannot persist and the upward pressure on money wages would restore the initial equilibrium. This is in accordance with the Classical theory.

Suppose, however, that the real wage had become stuck above the market-clearing level with initial money wage W_0 and lower price level P_1, depicted as W_0/P_1 in Figure 6.5. At this position there is an excess supply of labour. If the money wage were flexible, this would exert downward pressure and restore equilibrium. Since, according to Keynes, this is not the case, a labour market disequilibrium will persist. Employment will be at N_1 since employers will only employ the quantity of labour they demand. The quantity of labour available is N'_1 giving a level of involuntary unemployment of $N'_1 - N_1$.

The implications of this for the *ASS* are easily verified (see Figure 6.6). The labour market equilibrium W_0/P_0, N_0 in Figure 6.5 is identical to that of the Classical model. An increase in the price level lowers real wages, creating excess demand for labour. This is only short-lived and employment level N_0, and hence real income Y_0, is quickly restored at a higher price level, say P_2 in Figure 6.6; again this is akin to the Classical view expressed earlier, though the speed of adjustment is presumed to be slower.

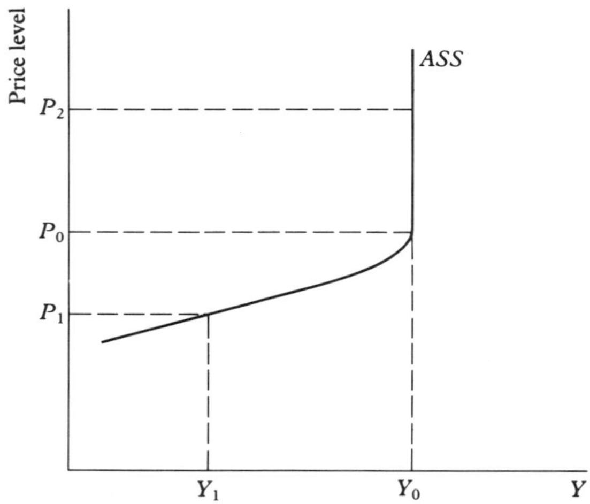

Figure 6.6 *The Keynesian aggregate supply schedule*

When the price level falls to P_1, however, real wages rise, creating excess supply and employment level N_1 in Figure 6.5. Since this is less than N_0, real income produced is also less, implying that below price level P_0 lower prices are associated with lower levels of output or real income. This gives point P_1, Y_1 in Figure 6.6.

Combining the *ASS* and *ADS* gives the determination of the price level in the Keynesian model (see Figure 6.7). Equilibrium is at point E_0, income level Y_0 and price level P_0 in Figure 6.7(b).

Figure 6.7(a) shows the *IS–LM* equilibrium, as a reminder that the points on the *ADS* correspond to *IS–LM* equilibrium values. It is now possible to determine equilibrium values for the rate of interest, real income and the price level.

POLICY IMPLICATIONS

The essence of Keynesian economics is the management of demand. It is clear from Figure 6.7 that movements in the demand curve no

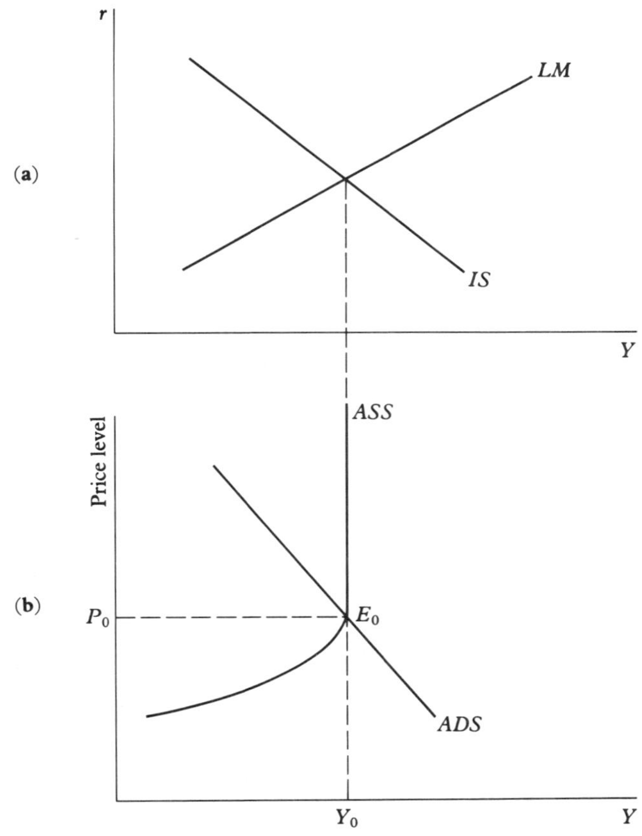

Figure 6.7 *Determination of the price level: The Keynesian case*

longer have unqualified policy implications. At levels of income below Y_0 demand management is capable of stimulating economic activity and raising real income. This comes about by reducing the level of excess supply and hence involuntary unemployment in the labour market. This may be accompanied by rising prices as indicated in the diagrams here, but Keynesian authors tended to play down this fact, implicitly assuming that the portion of the *ASS* to the left of Y_0 was flat, or completely 'price elastic'.

At levels of output beyond Y_0 Keynesians agree with the Classical analysis. Demand management is incapable of raising equilibrium income beyond the 'full employment' level as a *permanent* phenomenon. However, this raises the question: To what extent may an increase in aggregate demand temporarily raise income above the labour market equilibrium? In the Classical model the answer to this question is straightforward. Flexible markets ensure that an equilibrium is quickly reached. Keynesian economists cast doubt on this. While acknowledging that prices would be bid up, they question the speed at which this would happen. If markets, and particularly the labour market, are such that prices and wages adjust only slowly, it is possible that a situation of excess demand and hence higher employment may pertain for some significant length of time.

At this point it is worth re-emphasizing that *full employment* is used to refer to equilibrium in the labour market. This is not a political or social definition of full employment. Thus, for instance, it may be felt politically unacceptable to allow unemployment to rise above, say 3 per cent of the working population. It would only be by chance that labour market conditions would bring this about as a natural state of affairs. This possibility is illustrated by Figure 6.8.

Assume that the economy is currently in equilibrium at position P_0, Y_0. This corresponds to an underlying labour market equilibrium. A new government is elected and pledges to reduce unemployment to a 'politically acceptable' level associated with real income Y_p. The *IS–LM* framework demonstrates how Y_p may be achieved by an appropriate mixture of fiscal and monetary expansion.

The diagram illustrates an example of a monetary expansion to LM_1. This creates the familiar conditions, lowering interest rates and boosting aggregate demand to the required level. However, this position is not a full equilibrium; it is only partial in that equilibrium income and interest rates are achieved but not an equilibrium price level.

This is easily seen by representing the new higher level of aggregate

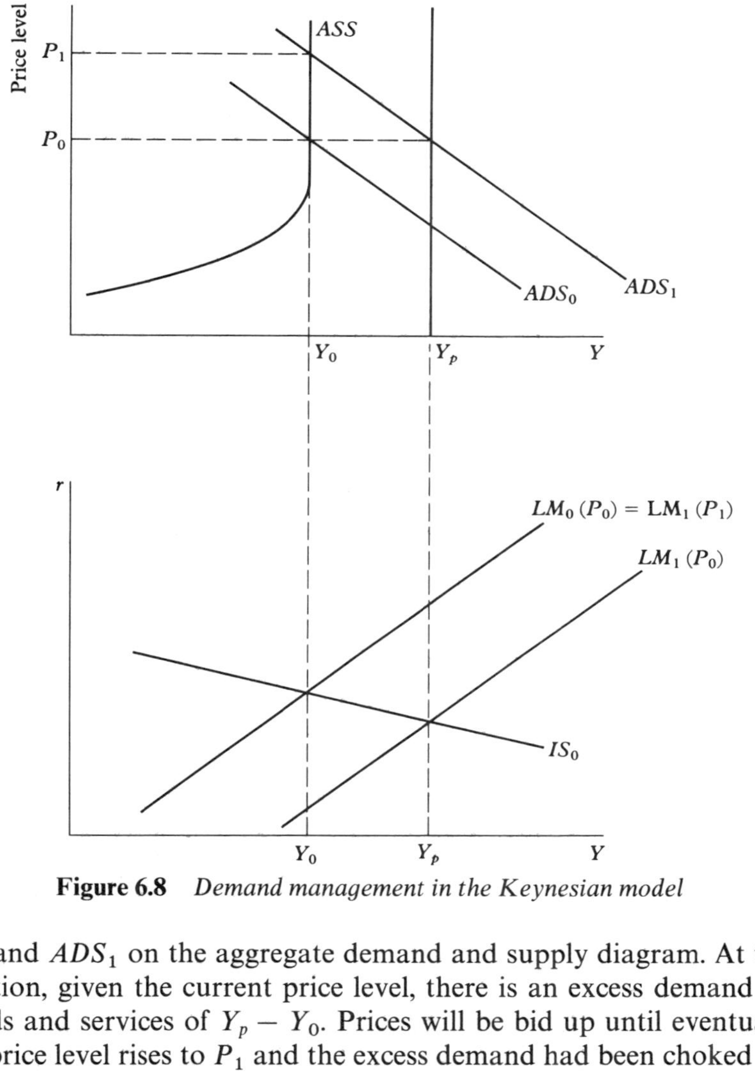

Figure 6.8 *Demand management in the Keynesian model*

demand ADS_1 on the aggregate demand and supply diagram. At this position, given the current price level, there is an excess demand for goods and services of $Y_p - Y_0$. Prices will be bid up until eventually the price level rises to P_1 and the excess demand had been choked off. The price level increase also reduces the real money supply, shifting *LM* back to the natural equilibrium position of Y_0, LM_1 (P_1).

By questioning the speed of this adjustment process, Keynesian economists opened the possibility for governments to trade off short-run reductions in unemployment against price level increases.

These policies would still leave the natural equilibrium of the economy unaltered. The problem of bringing about a permanent reduction in unemployment and raising the natural level of real income has focused attention on the aggregate supply schedule. Policies designed to influence the *ASS* have become known as *supply-side economics.* The implications of *supply management* are relevant to all the modern schools of macroeconomic thought and are discussed later in the chapter.

Keynesians and the inflation—unemployment trade-off

Of crucial importance to the above description of the Keynesian equilibrium is the *speed at which markets adjust.* If the movement from P_0, Y_p to P_1, Y_0 in Figure 6.8 is rapid, there is obviously little to be gained from the demand management policy. The long-run cost of such a policy, the higher price level, outweighs any short-run gain. If markets are inflexible, however, and it takes time to regain a new equilibrium, there is a short-term benefit from creating excess demand in the economy. In particular it raises the possibility of 'trading-off' lower unemployment against higher inflation. This trade-off is central to the Keynesian thesis. It was formalized and given apparent statistical backing by A. W. Phillips in 1958 and became enshrined in the curve which bears his name (see Figure 6.9).

In its original format, as developed by Phillips and later economists such as R. Lipsey, the trade-off was presumed to be permanent; rates of unemployment below U_0 would lead to persistent positive rates of inflation. The later emphasis placed on the speed of adjustment of the labour market implied that the trade-off would only be temporary, lasting only until the labour market had regained its equilibrium position.

In Figure 6.9 the long-run unemployment rate is U_0; this is consistent with employment N_0, Y_0 in Figure 6.7. The economy is in full equilibrium with a stable price level. Now suppose the government again attempts to achieve the acceptable income level Y_p with the associated level of unemployment U_p. Employment will rise and the level of money wages will be bid up. There is disequilibrium in the labour market. The rising wages will eventually be passed on in terms of higher prices and so a temporary inflation is generated. The economy moves to position I_p, U_p. The upward pressure on prices will reduce the real money supply, moving the *LM* schedule up (see Figure 6.8). Interest rates will rise and aggregate demand will start to fall. As a consequence the demand for labour is reduced once the labour market starts to return to its original equilibrium. The economy slides back

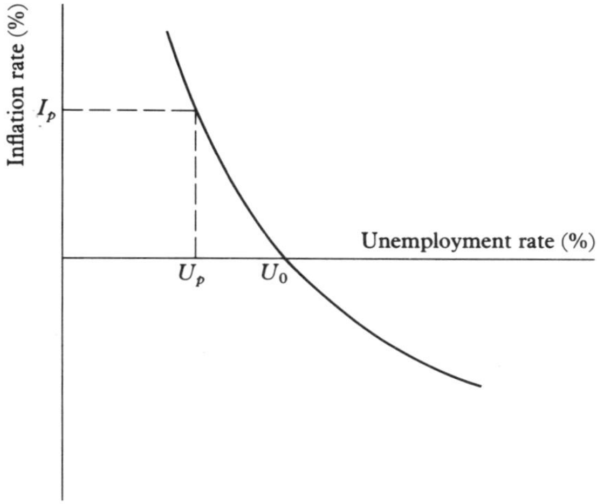

Figure 6.9 *The Phillips curve*

down the Phillips curve to U_0 with, as we have seen, a higher but *stable* price level. Thus a once-and-for-all expansion does not bring about a permanent trade-off of lower unemployment for higher inflation.

To summarize, the policy conclusions of the Keynesian and Classical models stand in stark contrast. Flexible markets and rapid adjustment in the Classical model render any form of demand management impotent. Wage rigidity and sluggishness of markets to adjust in the Keynesian model justify demand management under conditions of persistent disequilibrium.

This Keynesian view became prominent in political decision-taking throughout the 1960s on both sides of the Atlantic. Moreover actual experience appeared to support the Phillips relationship and the 'menu' of choices it offered governments in solving the problems of inflation and unemployment.

This view did not go unchallenged. During the late 1960s a group of economists led by Milton Friedman at the University of Chicago were attempting to show that fluctuations in economic activity were more highly correlated with variations in money supply than with fiscal demand management policies. The basis of this work was a reformulation of the Classical quantity theory of money which is why economists adhering to their views became known as 'Modern Monetarists' or just Monetarists.

In addition they also cast doubts on the practical operation of Keynesian demand management, pointing out that such a policy requires a detailed knowledge of the current position of the economy, the speed at which adjustment is taking place and the exact level of fiscal and monetary stimuli required to achieve a desired position on the Phillips curve. Monetarists claim that to assume access to such information is unrealistic, a point taken up in more detail in Chapter 8.

The simultaneous occurrence of high inflation and high unemployment in the 1970s and 1980s highlighted the weaknesses of the Keynesian model as presented so far. The Phillips relationship appeared to have broken down. The economy was reverting to its natural level of unemployment but with accelerating inflation. To explain these new conditions, opponents of the Keynesian view turned to the role of *expectation formation* by individuals. Given that individuals or their representatives, for example in the form of trade unions, have access to economic information about price levels, wage rates, interest rates and the like, they will form expectations of future events and attempt to protect the real wage of their members. For example, a union foreseeing an inflation rate of 10 per cent will attempt to negotiate a pay settlement which insulates them from any previously unforeseen inflation and from that which is expected. This would be in addition to any 'real' increase they attempt to win. Such behaviour is completely logical given the objectives of any trade grouping.

Expectations play a central role in macroeconomics, but because they cannot be observed in practice it is only recently that they have been incorporated in the theory. Keynes wrote at length about expectations, but ironically it is in reformulations of the Classical model that the major developments have taken place. Two views have emerged, namely, *adaptive expectations* and *rational expectations*. The former is associated with the Modern Monetarists, whilst the latter is a development of the New Classical school.

Adaptive expectations and the modern monetarists

The *adaptive expectations hypothesis* proposes that individuals update their forecasts of economic values like price inflation on the basis of the mistakes made in previous forecasts. If actual inflation is higher than that previously predicted, then forecasts of future inflation will be revised upwards. This process of adaptation does not simply refer to the last forecast error, however; the errors made in preceeding time periods are also taken into account. It is assumed that the further into the past an error was made, the less weight will be attributed to it in the present decision or prediction. The influence of previous over current expectations diminishes over time.

Consider the example of the expected rate of inflation $I^e{}_{t+1}$ made at time t. The model may be formalized as:

$$I^e{}_{t+1} = I^e{}_t + \beta(I_t - I^e{}_t); \quad 0 \leqslant \beta \leqslant 1.$$

β is the 'coefficient of expectation' determining the extent to which $I^e{}_t$ is 'adapted'. The error between the actual and expected values is given by the term $(I_t - I^e{}_t)$.

This model may be rewritten for any time period. Thus $I^e{}_t$ may be expressed:

$$I^e{}_t = I^e{}_{t-1} + \beta(I_{t-1} - I^e{}_{t-1}).$$

It follows that $I^e{}_{t+1}$ is based on both $I^e{}_t$ and $I^e{}_{t-1}$. Similarly $I^e{}_{t-1}$ could be expressed in terms of $I^e{}_{t-2}$ and so on, which implies that the current expectation $I^e{}_{t+1}$ is based on all previous expectations, their influence on the current expectation diminishing over time. This demonstrates both an intuitive quality and a fundamental weakness of the model. Individuals learn from previous experience rather than having no memory, but this learning is entirely retrospective. Any current facts and information are completely ignored by the adaptive expectations hypothesis.

To consider the implications of this hypothesis for the Phillips relationship, suppose that the economy is currently in long-run equilibrium and has been so for some considerable time. Unemployment is at the natural rate and there will be zero price inflation; thus the expected rate of inflation is also zero. The government now attempts to reduce unemployment by a policy of, say, a sustained increase in the rate of monetary growth. This implies that the nominal money stock will not be constant in the long run.

The situation is set out in Figure 6.10. The initial Phillips curve is PC_0. The monetary expansion results in labour market disequilibrium, increasing employment until eventually the economy moves up PC_0 to position I_p, U_p. Inflationary expectations will be adjusted upward. If $I_p = 10$ per cent and $\beta = 1$, the expected rate of inflation in the future is 10 per cent; there are no previous errors to adapt this, since prices have been stable over time and previous predictions have been correct.

As wage contracts come up for renewal, labour will attempt to

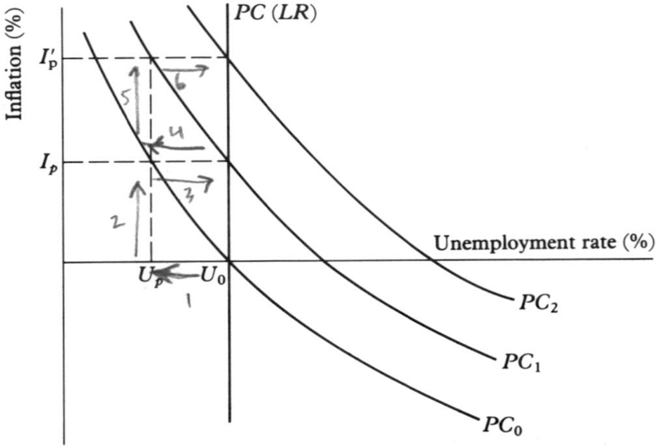

Figure 6.10 *The Monetarist long-run Phillips curve*

regain its original *real wage*. The rising real wage will again increase unemployment to U_0, the natural rate, but now at an inflation rate of I_p per cent on PC_1. The economy will move back to its original rate of unemployment but at a higher rate of actual and expected inflation.

If the government again attempts to attain U_p it will generate I'_p on PC_2, which in turn becomes the expected rate of inflation and by means of the re-establishment of the real wage is eventually associated with U_0. Thus, the long-run or equilibrium Phillips curve relationship is a vertical line at U_0, denoted in Figure 6.10 as *PC*(*LR*). There is a temporary trade-off between inflation and unemployment but there is no permanent trade-off. The short-run trade-off which does occur stems not from the inflation *per se*, but from *unanticipated* inflation. This in general requires a rising rate of inflation, rather than just a high rate. Repeated attempts to reduce unemployment below the natural rate will result in a higher inflation rate.

By emphasizing the role of expectations the Monetarists made clear the possibility of short-run losses from policies designed to stimulate demand and also concluded that there were no long-term gains.

The policy implications of this are summarized in Figure 6.11. The increase in aggregate demand from ADS_0 to ADS_1 will eventually result in $P_1 Y_0$. The short-run outcome occurs because some of the inflation generated is not fully anticipated, and there is a temporary fall in real wages, hence the positively sloped short-run aggregate supply schedule *ASS*(*SR*). The long-run schedule is thus the *correctly antici-*

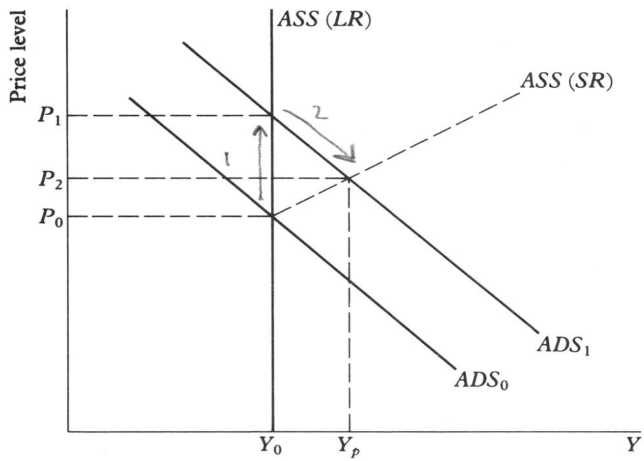

Figure 6.11 *Demand management: The Monetarist case*

pated inflation curve. The conclusion that demand management is ineffective implied that, to reduce unemployment, policies should be focused on the objective of easing labour market conditions and increasing productivity. Modern Monetarists drew attention to the supply side of the macroeconomy.

Rational expectations and the New Classical school

The adaptive expectations model has a major weakness as a description of human behaviour in that it ignores current events. For instance, current inflationary expectations would be left unaltered by changes in government policy which individuals knew would influence the price level. Thus if the adaptive expectation of inflation were 10 per cent but the government had just announced that it was doubling the rate of monetary growth to, say, 20 per cent, there would be an immediate effect on inflation, but according to the model the expectation of 10 per cent would remain unaltered. Similarly, in the following period expected inflation would be revised upwards in response to the previous forecast error, while the government may have announced a 75 per cent reduction in the growth of the money supply.

It would be expected that people would use all the available information they have in forming their expectations. When people behave in this manner they are obeying the *rational expectations hypothesis.*

This hypothesis, along with the assumption of highly flexible and quickly adjusting markets characteristic of the old Classical school, characterizes the New Classical macroeconomics.

Since available information is imperfect, the rational expectations hypothesis does not preclude errors in individuals' forecasts of economic events, but it does imply that they will not continue to make systematic errors as indicated by the adaptive expectations hypothesis. Any unforeseen expectational errors will be fully incorporated into the information set on which a new expectation will be formed. To make consistent systematic errors is irrational.

Consider, for example, a trade union negotiating a new wage contract for its members. Both unions and employers form rational expectations of the future rate of price changes and set a money increase sufficient to offset the price rise, thus maintaining the real wage. If the actual rate of inflation turns out to be identical to that expected, then the market remains in equilibrium. Any disparity will cause a labour market disequilibrium. If actual inflation is above that anticipated, then employers gain, and output rises. If it is lower, it will favour labour but will reduce short-run employment because of the rise in real wages. The next time the money wage is set, this information enters the expectation formation and the relevant adjustments are made. It is only the custom of annual or periodic wage contracts which prevents an immediate renegotiation of the wage rate in the event of a disparity between actual and previously expected values.

In the context of this example, if the above increase in monetary growth is announced, then it is assumed that both employers and unions take it into account when setting the wage rate. Both are aware of the consequences of accelerated monetary growth through experience or otherwise. The consequences of rising prices are incorporated into the negotiations and a higher money wage is set. If this behaviour is generalized across the economy, the monetary expansion has no effect on real variables because all agents make adequate compensation.

The results may be characterized by the familiar aggregate supply and demand model in Figure 6.12. The *ASS* is upward sloping because of the possibility of unanticipated expectational errors. A government policy to boost aggregate demand shifts the *ADS* from ADS_0 to ADS_1. There is, however, no trade-off between higher output and higher prices or, in terms of the Phillips curve, lower unemployment and higher inflation. Wage contracts are renegotiated at the earliest oppor-

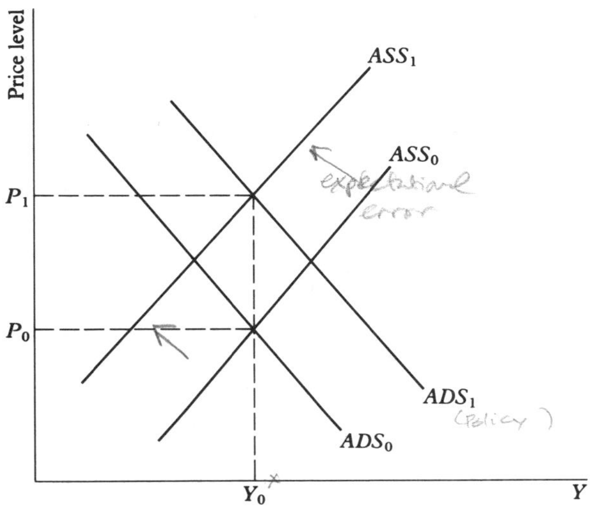

Figure 6.12 *The New Classical model*

tunity, re-establishing the labour market equilibrium. This moves the economy back to Y_0 by an upward shift in the ASS to ASS_1.

Any pre-announced policy will be negated in the same way. Changes by government which are not anticipated by economic decision-takers will cause some short-term trade-off, but agents soon become aware of them and in the absence of any other changes equilibrium is quickly restored.

In this context the role of demand-orientated policy should be limited to providing a stable environment for the economy. It should avoid rapid changes in the rate of monetary growth, because this would lead to variations in the rate of inflation. An unstable rate of inflation is more likely to lead to expectational error. Stable values for the nominal variables in the economy would reduce expectational error and thus minimize any short-run deviation of the economy from its natural equilibrium.

Active policy again emphasizes the supply-side of the economy, although this time the conclusion stems from an equilibrium model, that is, one of rapid adjustment, rather than a disequilibrium model as is the case in both the Keynesian and Modern Monetarist theories.

Supply-side economics

Modern theories of the macroeconomy have shifted emphasis away from demand management towards influencing the supply conditions of the economy. The so-called *supply-side economics* refer to microeconomic policies designed to increase the natural level, or equilibrium level, of output. This is largely determined by conditions in the labour market and the way in which capital and labour are combined in the production process. It is towards influencing these areas that recent policy in the UK and USA has been primarily directed.

The labour market equilibrium will be affected by either an increased willingness to work or the desire to employ more workers. To this end governments have attempted to make work more attractive. For instance, it has been suggested that cuts in the marginal rate of income tax improve incentives by raising the take-home pay while not increasing the cost to the employer. Similarly, policies have been directed toward reducing the non-wage cost to employers in terms of national insurance payments.

A more politically sensitive issue is the structure and level of unemployment benefits. It is argued that if these are set too high they deter individuals from work by making it financially less attractive. Trade unions are also seen as having adverse effects on the level of employment by imposing closed-shop arrangements and reducing the mobility of labour between jobs.

Policies designed to affect the demand side of the labour market tend to be interrelated with those to improve the overall productive capacity. Investment in new machinery is encouraged as are technological progress and its innovation.

Additional reading

There is a vast literature on the areas discussed in this chapter. Those below represent only a very limited selection. A good guide to further references may be obtained from the bibliographies of those listed here.

1. Hicks, J. 'What is Wrong with Monetarism?' *Lloyds Bank Review*, October 1975.
2. Kaldor, N. 'The New Monetarism', *Lloyds Bank Review*, July 1970.
3. Klamer, A. (1984) *The New Classical Macroeconomics*, Wheatsheaf.
4. Laidler, D. 'Monetarism: An Interpretation and Assessment', *Economic Journal*, 1981.
5. Laidler, D. and Parkin, J. 'Inflation: A Survey', *Economic Journal*, 1975.
6. Minford, P. (1985) *Unemployment: Cause and Cure*, Basil Blackwell.
7. Phillips, A. W. 'The Relationship Between Unemployment and the Rate

of Change of Money Wages in the UK, 1861–1957', in M. G. Meuller, *Readings in Macroeconomics*, 2nd edn, Holt International, 1971.
8. Sawyer, M. C. (1982) *Macroeconomics in Question*, Wheatsheaf.
9. Shaw, G. K. (1984) *Rational Expectation*, Wheatsheaf. (A highly readable introduction to the theory and implication of the rational expectations hypothesis.)

7.

The main policy implications

The main economic objectives of government were outlined in Chapter 1. It is towards the achievement of these aims that policies are directed. To recall these aims, they are:

1. A 'satisfactory' rate of economic growth
2. A stable price level
3. A low level of unemployed resources
4. A 'satisfactory' balance of payments
5. A stable currency

The preceding analysis of Chapters 5 and 6 reveals some of the major divergences of view between Keynesian, Monetarist and New Classical economists. These differences emerge particularly clearly from a consideration of the main policy stance adopted by each school.

Keynesians

Central to Keynesian analysis is the notion of market imperfections and market failure. Markets in general and the labour market in particular fail to adjust quickly to changing conditions, and thus never reach equilibrium. Keynesians believe that government can and should respond to these shortcomings of the market mechanism by implementing demand management policies. These may involve the use of fiscal and/or monetary policy to make short-run adjustments to the level of aggregate demand and, through it, the level of income and employment. Such policies might include fiscal expansion, for example, by increasing government expenditure on the economic infrastructure, improving roads and other forms of communication. They could involve an expansion of the money supply through government buying securities from the public and thus paying money out into circulation, the aim being to stimulate private investment by lowering the rate of interest.

This emphasis upon regular intervention to cater for market imperfections and slow adjustment implies that the Keynesian concern is focused upon short-run economic management in a condition of perpetual disequilibrium. Policies may be short term in duration, but the overall longer-term effect is achieved by continual reappraisal and adjustment: fiscal and monetary policies are regularly updated.

Keynesians believe that it is possible and beneficial to trade off objectives like inflation and unemployment. Due to market imperfections introduced by institutional structures, such as trade unions and the welfare state, any demand management policy runs the risk of generating inflation. It may be necessary to implement a prices and incomes policy to avoid an upward spiral of labour costs and prices.

Much importance is attributed to the role of external events in influencing the course which an economy follows. For example, the occurrence of both rapid inflation and high unemployment in the mid-1970s was considered to be the result of oil price rises which both raised prices and lowered demand. In this environment of 'stagflation' people accepted inflation as a norm which they incorporated in their expectations. Such expectations are difficult to revise as inflation is built into both wages and prices.

Keynesians also believe that supply-side policies to raise productivity are appropriate as a means of raising total output. At full employment this would constitute the only means by which total production could be permanently raised. It is important to recognize, however, that they do not accept the notion of an automatic or natural tendency for the economy to move towards, or be at, full employment.

Demand-side policies may also have beneficial supply-side effects, e.g., if the lowering of interest rates cited earlier succeeded in raising private investment, this could increase both employment and the production of capital goods and services, raising productive potential.

The main emphasis in the Keynesian system is upon short-term demand management policies while also acknowledging the contribution which supply-side policies can make to increasing potential output.

Monetarists

Unlike the Keynesians, the Monetarists view full employment equilibrium output as the norm, from which the economy may often diverge but towards which it will tend naturally. The slow process of market adjustment in the Keynesian model is replaced by a faster one which obviates the need for government-inspired demand management. The economy may operate in conditions of disequilibrium but, if left to operate as freely as institutional rigidities will allow, the market mechanism will surpass government efforts to achieve full employment.

Monetarists do not, therefore, consider an active role by government in economic management to be either necessary or desirable. In their view, government failure is just as likely and potentially more damaging than the market failure referred to in Chapter 1. The Keynesian argument for a growing role of government in the economy is regarded as undesirable, since it simply raises the probability of policy imperfections and failure.

Much reliance is placed upon the market mechanism to allocate and reallocate factors of production. The level of employment and hence output is determined by the real wage rate, which is in turn subject to the operation of institutions which impinge upon the labour market.

Institutionally based distortions may arise from several sources. For example, trade unions may effectively resist reductions in wages; welfare payments may reduce the number of people prepared to work; high direct taxation may constitute a disincentive to working harder for greater remuneration.

Output may also be affected by changes such as advances in technology, the innovation of new techniques and the birth of more new enterprises. Supply-side policies frequently focus on these sources of potential growth.

Aside from once-and-for-all reductions in direct taxation to raise incentives, fiscal policy serves simply as a means of raising funds to enable government expenditure. Frequent changes in fiscal policy for the purposes of demand management are viewed as a source of instability which introduces more uncertainty for economic decision-takers in forming their expectations.

Monetary policy is also seen to perform a very different role from the Keynesian strategy of demand management. The role of money is entirely neutral. It determines the price level and hence nominal as opposed to real values. Changes in the rate of monetary growth can have no lasting effect upon output. A reduction in the rate of monetary growth is necessary to reduce inflation, and its effectiveness is in part determined by the strength of resolve of the monetary authorities.

Inflationary expectations will be formed more accurately and with greater certainty if people are more convinced that the monetary growth rate targets announced by government are realistic and will be strictly adhered to. The greater the credibility of the government's monetary strategy, the larger will be the effect upon inflationary expectations and the more incentive there is for price and wage setters to adjust their behaviour. Where this is the case, the inflation is only short lived.

The overriding emphasis in the Monetarist system is upon stability. Monetary and fiscal policies are designed to help achieve this aim. Fiscal policy finances the minimal and stable role of government in the economy, while monetary policy is used to ensure steady monetary growth in line with real income. Output growth is encouraged through the implementation of supply-side policies to aid the free operation of the market and promote new enterprise and innovation.

New Classicals

The policy conclusions of the New Classical school are broadly similar to those of the Monetarists, though there are certain fundamental differences in the way they are reached.

Keynesians perceive a sufficiently significant time lag in market adjustment for a state of perpetual disequilibrium to exist. Monetarists disagree on the size of the time lag, viewing market conditions to be much closer to a natural equilibrium. New Classical economists believe the time lag in adjustment to be so short that the economy is, to all intents and purposes, in a condition of perpetual, if changing, equilibrium. Prevailing prices are such as to clear the market and 'full employment' is the norm; there is only voluntary unemployment given existing real wage levels.

Under the New Classical conditions government is powerless to affect the level of output through demand management; it is subject to *policy ineffectiveness*. Any attempt to influence demand and output will be quickly perceived, expected and incorporated by price and wage setters. Only unforeseen demand changes can influence output, and the effect will be temporary, as economic decisions will quickly adjust and accommodate.

Deviations from the 'natural' level of output can also occur through imperfect information: a policy change may not be perfectly foreseen by economic decision takers. Mistakes and misconceptions are therefore inevitable, even though decisions are rational, given the information available.

As in the Monetarist case, the policy prescription of the New Classical school is one of supply-side management to raise the natural level of production. The main role of government is to provide a stable environment to enable the accurate setting of expectations. They should attempt to reduce uncertainty by indicating, as much as is practically possible, the future course of monetary growth and economic activity. The principal aim is to minimize errors in the formation of expectations and thus reduce the incidence of deviations from the 'natural' level of output and employment.

Having observed the contrasting policy prescriptions which emerge from the different schools in abstract, it is necessary to appreciate various constraints to which they are subject when applied in practice.

It is clear that the nature of macroeconomic policy advice varies considerably according to the particular theoretical stance taken. As indicated at the beginning of this book, however, prevailing economic conditions and policies reflect the posture not only of existing but also of previous governments. Economies cannot be swiftly converted to a radically different industrial structure. Governments inheriting a large public sector, for example, may adhere strongly to a non-interventionist stance such as that proposed by the Monetarists and New Classicals. The actual process of extricating themselves from commitments made by preceding governments is both difficult and time consuming. As a result much of the economic intervention undertaken by governments is largely determined by the actions of previous governments. It is these actions that both define existing commitments and influence prevailing conditions. There is therefore a clear distinction between a change in conventionally accepted economic theory and its reflection in a different role of government in the economy.

These points are clearly demonstrated in the experience of the UK since the late 1970s where a more overt supply-side approach has been adopted. The application of Keynesian doctrine in the 1950s and 1960s created an institutional infrastructure and a large role of government in the economy which still dominates much government activity. The application of Monetarist and/or New Classical policies has been prohibited by an inability to avoid an essentially interventionist role. As a result it is unclear whether the fall in inflation rates, for example, should be attributed to a tighter, more predictable monetary policy, or to the effective deflation in economic activity which that caused. The fall in inflation can be interpreted either as a benefit of the supply-side approach or as a simple Keynesian deflation.

Despite these general points on the ability of governments to make fundamental changes, most still attempt to influence the course of the economy, if by different routes.

The Keynesian emphasis is upon counteracting the natural cycles which are perceived as characterizing economic activity, in order to avoid excessive unemployment in a recession and price inflation in a boom. Monetarists and New Classical economists also aim to avoid fluctuations in output and employment, though they perceive these as deviations from natural equilibrium levels rather than any inbuilt tendency towards cyclical behaviour.

As a result, in part, of the pre-eminence of Keynesian doctrine in the 1950s and 1960s government is still, therefore, involved in economic management. Regular budgets are introduced and attempts are made to evaluate the implications of the strategies adopted, by recourse to complex econometric models such as that used by the Treasury.

The actual process of government intervention is subject to many problems, owing to the dynamic nature of economic activity referred to in Chapter 1. Time lags, external events and information deficiencies mean that government actions are, for the economy, imprecise and uncertain in terms of their likely outcome.

The final chapter of the book considers some of the main sources of difficulty when attempting to decide on the appropriate form of government intervention. The points covered are accompanied by reference to the 'Chancellor' game mentioned at the end of Chapter 1. The aim is to convey some of the main problems of macroeconomic policy in practice. Where it is available, recourse to the 'Chancellor' game can contribute further to an understanding of these problems by enabling users to experience elements of the decision-making process themselves.

Additional reading

1. Friedman, M. 'The Role of Monetary Policy', *American Economic Review*, 1968.
2. Hicks, J. 'What is Wrong with Monetarism?' *Lloyds Bank Review*, October 1975.
3. Kaldor, N. 'The New Monetarism', *Lloyds Bank Review*, July 1970.

4. Klamer, A. (1984) *The New Classical Macroeconomics*, Wheatsheaf.
5. Laidler, D. 'Monetarism: An Interpretation and Assessment', *Economic Journal*, 1981.
6. Laidler, D. and Parkin, J. 'Inflation: A Survey', *Economic Journal*, 1975.
7. Minford, P. (1985) *Unemployment: Cause and Cure*, Basil Blackwell.
8. Modigliani, F. (1985) *The Debate over Stabilization Policies and other Macroeconomic Issues*, Cambridge University Press.
9. Phillips, A. W. 'The Relationship Between Unemployment and the Rate of Change of Money Wages in the UK, 1861–1957,' in M.G. Mueller, *Readings in Macroeconomics*, 2nd edn, Holt International, 1971.
10. Sawyer, M. C. (1982) *Macroeconomics in Question*, Wheatsheaf.
11. Shaw, G. K. (1984) *Rational Expectations*, Wheatsheaf.

8.

Practical problems of economic control

The application of macroeconomic policy is confronted by a number of problems. Some of these refer to both demand and supply-side initiatives, while others reflect the differential emphases placed upon specific economic variables by the different schools of thought.

Consideration here is given first to the problems which affect intervention in general and second to more specific difficulties encountered by opposing doctrines. This is followed by a brief consideration of the process of market adjustment, since it is around the speed of this process that much contemporary debate revolves.

Time lags

Governments are constrained by a set of interrelated time lags characterizing policy. First, there is a delay in recognition of the need for intervention, because information about the economy is not immediate. A government might wish to counteract economic cycles, but fail to do so successfully because the information required to anticipate cyclical events is unavailable.

Second, there is a delay in implementing policy due to the administrative and organizational aspects of its design and application. This time lag varies according to the nature of the intervention. For example, changes in taxation can be made rapidly, while the introduction of new employment legislation may be time consuming.

Third, there is a delay in the effect of policy; again this will vary between different policies. In addition to this time lag it is often the case that the actual effect is different from the objective. This may be so for a variety of reasons, such as incorrect policy design due to imperfect information, unanticipated exogenous events like exchange rate fluctuations, and so forth. In the event of undesirable side-effects from previous policies, there will tend to be a recognition lag, as indicated above. The perception of a need to intervene, the design of policy, its implementation and actual effects, are all characterized by time lags and uncertainty. Given the dynamic nature of economies, policies designed in response to one situation will be implemented in another. This may severely reduce the potency of government policy in economic management.

Many of the relationships in the 'Chancellor' game are characterized by time lags. The user may be unable to reverse swiftly the effects of a previous initiative: a change in strategy will often take time to become effective and the effects will often be different from those anticipated. It is in part for this reason that the user is confronted by several consecutive years of economic control in order to fully realize the problems involved. The user is also provided with an indication of the previous five years' economic experience on commencing the game and while playing it; this too is designed to highlight the dynamic and time-lagged nature of economic intervention.

Exogenous events

Government policy will also be affected by events and policies in other countries. Domestic policies may arise in response to these exogenous factors; similarly, the actual outcome of political initiatives may be altered by them.

The significance which is attributed to exogenous shocks as economic influences depends largely upon the speed at which the economy is assumed to adjust. As was made clear in Chapter 6 and is discussed further in this chapter, the speed of economic adjustment is crucial to the debate as to the desirability of economic intervention by government. This is true in the case of outside economic influences. If adjustment is relatively slow, as the Keynesians argue, then the nature of intervention will tend to change in response to the effects of external events. If markets adjust relatively quickly or almost instantaneously, as the Monetarists and New Classical school respectively believe, then intervention is not only unnecessary but potentially damaging as a source of further market distortion.

Whether adjustment is slow or fast the dramatic economic impact of exogenous events is clear, dwarfing the effects of domestic policy. As indicated earlier, the world recession of 1975 was largely attributed to the oil price escalation introduced by OPEC, initially in 1973. Further

OPEC price rises alongside a general tightening of monetary and fiscal policy to control countries' public expenditure were blamed for the recession in 1981–82.

Individual countries were powerless to isolate themselves from these and other events; the debate concerns the extent to which intervention could and can be used to mitigate against the effects. Monetarists and New Classical economists would in theory advocate a policy of non-intervention, thus allowing the market mechanism to make the requisite adjustments. Keynesians propose policies aimed at negating the impact of outside influences directly, without relying solely on market forces. As is indicated in Chapter 7, most governments are obliged to adopt an interventionist stance, because of the large role of the public sector, created in part by the earlier application of Keynesian policies.

Intervention is complicated not only by the time lags described above, but also by a frequent shortage of accurate, up-to-date information. The task of economic control presented to the user of the 'Chancellor' game is made easier than that which confronts Chancellors of the Exchequer. External shocks to the economy are not included and much information is provided which would, in practice, require careful interpretation because of the possible errors involved. The game is designed to convey clearly some of the main possible policy trade-offs in intervention. The incorporation of exogenous shocks and deliberate misinformation would tend to obscure these relationships and thus lower the educational value of the game by reducing the need for analysis and increasing that of guesswork. Many of the benefits derived from using the game arise from a consideration of the possible implications of different strategies. Some uncertainty is introduced by the inclusion of random elements in the external sector of the model. It was, however, considered important to retain an overall consistency in order to encourage analysis rather than discourage it by the frequent introduction of fundamental changes in conditions outside the control of the user. Nonetheless it is also important to appreciate the problems presented to government owing to a lack of reliable and accurate information.

Information, measurement and definition

Information is needed to verify and apply the various opposing theoretical positions described in Chapter 6. The main problems arise from the difficulties of definition, measurement and collection at an aggregate level. Owing to the nature of the subject matter, the information available is often unreliable and out of date. These points emerge more clearly from a consideration of the specific problems and information requirements of the three main schools of thought.

THE KEYNESIAN POSITION

If dynamic economic activity can be realistically set within a cyclical framework, then an element of predictability is introduced so long as the economy's position in the cycle is known. This is only useful to government, therefore, if reliable information on the main economic indicators is available for several years.

The measurement of many of the aggregates concerned is highly imperfect, thus introducing the potential for errors in judgement as to the requisite changes in aggregate demand. For example, the calculation of national income and unemployment faces many potential sources of error, such as the operation of the 'Black Economy'; the magnitude of such errors is difficult to ascertain. The 'rate of inflation' refers to changes in the average price level based upon the price changes of a specific set of goods and services; it is in part determined by the choice of goods and services and the manner by which they are included in the calculation.

In addition to the many problems of calculating macroeconomic aggregates and their rates of change, Keynesians confront further difficulties because of their reliance upon econometric models of the economy. These models are used to facilitate demand management by providing information about the potential implications of different policy strategies. Many opponents of demand management argue that the 'state of the art' in macroeconomic simulation modelling is insufficiently accurate or reliable to justify the use of such models. The specification and estimation of the many economic relationships which these systems require may reflect more the particular theoretical bias of the modellers rather than portraying how the economy actually operates. Like all computer-based systems, the resulting output of information reflects the nature of the input in terms of data and model structure.

Despite their rejection of econometric modelling as an aid to the design of demand management policies, many supply-side economists are obliged to consider the predictions provided by different models when deciding how to control the large public sector which exists in most developed mixed economies. The contradictory results yielded by different models represents an additional source of confusion to the government.

THE MONETARIST AND NEW CLASSICAL SCHOOLS

Both these schools of thought emphasize a linkage between the money supply and the price level. Inflation or changes in the average price level arise from discrepancies between the rate of growth of the money supply and real income. Expectations are seen to play a key role in determining economic decisions; the more stable the economy and particularly inflation, the more accurate will be expectations and the more stable, in turn, will be the economy. A central role of government in achieving such stability is that of controlling the money supply in the medium term (i.e., five years). The target rate of monetary growth is declared, and expectations can thus be formed more confidently as to the likely rate of change of prices.

In order to implement this kind of control successfully it is necessary to gain access to a reliable measure of the level and rate of growth of the money supply. Measuring and controlling the money supply is very difficult and therefore subject to the possibility of large margins of error. Although, as indicated earlier, several measures are used by governments in their attempts to gain an indication of the money supply, more accurate measures tend to refer to less useful indicators. The amount of money in the form of cash, notes and coinage in circulation can be estimated quite accurately. Changes in this measure do not necessarily reflect what is happening to the overall money supply when many other forms of credit and institutional accounts are introduced. Different measures of the money supply frequently yield conflicting predictions as to its rate of growth.

In its attempts to control the money supply, the UK Government has focused attention upon its own expenditure and consequent borrowing levels, the *public sector borrowing requirement* (PSBR). Short-term borrowing to finance the PSBR raises the money supply. Reductions in the growth rate or level of government expenditure may not reduce the PSBR, however, if they lead to deflation and higher unemployment. Under these conditions government loses tax revenues and may be committed to larger welfare expenditures to those newly unemployed; the PSBR rises as revenues fall and expenditures increase.

Although government can influence the money supply by imposing limits on its own borrowing and by controlling the net issue of cash, it is more difficult to regulate credit to the private sector. In the absence of a strong interventionist stance with respect to institutional credit creation, money supply levels and growth due to borrowing by the private sector is largely demand-determined. Credit is provided to individuals and firms in response to requests for loans by them, assuming they are deemed sufficiently credit-worthy. Government's attempts to constrain private sector borrowing, by using its considerable influence in money markets to raise interest rates, may have undesirable side effects as the exchange rate strengthens and private sector investment is discouraged. These detrimental repercussions are exacerbated if, as appears to be the case in the UK, borrowing is relatively insensitive to interest rate changes; interest rates may have to rise to unacceptably high levels to reduce the demand for credit. The unacceptability may be due, for example, to the rise in mortgage rates and the consequent rise in the rate of inflation this would represent.

Just as Monetarists envisage problems in portraying accurately the state and direction of the economy, so Keynesians in turn would claim that there is insufficient information referring to the money supply, or changes in it, to either verify Monetarist doctrine or apply it.

A second problem area for the Monetarist and New Classical schools of thought concerns their concept of a 'natural' level of unemployment for any given level of real wages. Each of these aggregates, unemployment and the real wage level, conceals wide variations in practice. Policies designed to affect the aggregate may have differential impacts upon the constitutent groups.

Unemployment varies by industry and region. It can be argued in theory that these differences reflect similar variations in the natural levels dictated by the prevailing real wage rates in each firm and area. This claim must remain theoretical, however, until the prodigious volume of information required to demonstrate it empirically becomes available. Where the industrial structure is changing, for example away from the staple industries such as steel and coal production, there may be increasing pressure to implement regional policies to relieve the high unemployment which results.

The unemployed are not a homogenous group. Some may be temporarily out of work between jobs, the short-term unemployed. Others may, after a year or more searching unsuccessfully for work, perceive no possibility of future employment. These long-term unemployed are effectively removed from the 'natural' level of unemployment, since, having given up searching, they no longer serve to apply downward pressure on the real wage rate. Keynesians argue that these individuals could be re-employed through demand management without applying any upward pressure on the real wage rate and, through it, prices.

There is in practice a wide distribution of real incomes between occupations. Again it is possible to argue that, in theory, these reflect different economic contributions. An overall objective of reducing the real wage rate does not specify whether this should be borne proportionately by everyone or disproportionately by some groups. There may be excess demand in some labour markets and excess supply in others, given the prevailing real wage distribution. The information required to ascertain the conditions in each market and therefore the appropriate changes, is considerable. Attempts to facilitate the market process may achieve an equitable result in theory, but again this cannot be verified in practice.

Market adjustment

In justifying the acceptance by government of their separate and contradictory interpretations of macroeconomic relationships, much emphasis is placed by the various opposing factions upon the speed of market adjustment. This area of disagreement focuses in particular upon the labour market.

Keynesians argue that adjustments to changing conditions will tend to be relatively slow owing to the many imperfections which characterize the productive operation of labour. These rigidities occur for a variety of reasons, both natural and deliberate. Labour mobility between industries and areas is naturally discouraged by the need to retrain or to move away from familiar and often closely built communities. It is deliberately constrained by rigid job demarcation and the operation of the 'closed shop'. Other aspects of labour organization, such as the strict maintenance of wage differentials, would be expected to impede market adjustment via labour mobility and relative real wage changes. Keynesians would argue that these market rigidities prevent adjustment. This absence of market flexibility would mean that the assumption of policy ineffectiveness made by New Classical economists no longer holds, since markets cannot adjust to accommodate policy changes and policies *will* have an effect.

Similarly, managerial ineptitude in perceiving and adapting to changes in the conditions of demand and production, the operation of an 'old boy' network as a means of allocating managerial jobs, and a lack of awareness of new technologies, would all be expected to frustrate the market mechanism and affect relative competitiveness.

While trying to reduce and minimize the undesirable consequences of such imperfections, Keynesians would argue that demand management policies should be used to move the economy towards the more desirable economic conditions which are obtainable. Both Monetarists and New Classical economists disagree with this Keynesian view of relatively slow market adjustment. They do not deny the existence of the rigidities and imperfections described above, but would simply claim that these underlie the prevailing positions of the aggregate labour demand and supply schedules.

For any given average real wage level there will be a corresponding level of natural unemployment as determined by the interaction of the demand and supply conditions. Alleviating market imperfections may shift either or both of these schedules. Adjustment is still claimed to occur relatively swiftly within this framework, however, through the operation of expectations. Demand management is unnecessary and unhelpful; only supply-side policies can have a lasting effect upon the level of economic activity.

To gain an insight into macroeconomic theory and policy it is necessary to understand the major changes in interpretation which have occurred. The rejection of the Classical model in favour of Keynesian doctrine through the 1950s and 1960s created the conditions under which Monetarists, New Classical economists and Keynesians argue in the 1980s. Despite the inertia in changing the economic role of government and the practical problems of intervention and altering its nature and effect, changes in conventionally accepted theory have been reflected gradually in policy. The movement away from demand management towards a more supply-side approach has been clearly observable in many Western developed mixed economies. A large element of government intervention still predominates, however, particularly in the United Kingdom.

Additional reading

The following is a list of commentaries and critiques on postwar demand management policies in the UK.

1. Beckerman, W. (ed.), *The Labour Government's Economic Record*, 1966–70, Duckworth.
2. Blackaby, F. T. (1978) *British Economic Policy*, 1960–74 Cambridge University Press.
3. Fforde, J. 'Setting Monetary Objectives', *Bank of England Quarterly Bulletin*, June 1983.
4. Keegan, W. (1984) *Mrs Thatcher's Economic Experiment*, Penguin.
5. Kennedy, M. C. 'The Economy as a Whole', in A. R. Prest and D. J. Coppock (eds.) *The UK Economy: A Manual of Applied Economics*, Weidenfeld and Nicolson, 1982.

9.

The 'Chancellor' game

This software places the user in the role of Chancellor of the Exchequer. It is designed to provide an insight to the decisions, trade-offs and uncertainties which characterize any attempt to control the course which an economy follows. The aims of macroeconomic policy refer to several interrelated objectives; the pursuit of any one of these will have repercussions for the others. The game contributes to a better comprehension of macroeconomics in several ways. First, it embodies many of the interrelationships which are relevant to the process of economic intervention as have been discussed throughout this book, and hence it reinforces an understanding of them, Second, it encourages players to use economic analysis by requiring them to decide upon a combination of policies in order to pursue a particular balance of objectives in terms of, for example, inflation, unemployment and economic growth. This decision-making process involves the application of the knowledge and understanding of macroeconomic relationships gained from this and other sources.

For the player the objective of the game is to manage an economy over an eight year period by manipulating five control variables, or means of intervention: the basic rate of income tax, the minimum lending rate, the rate of VAT, the level of government expenditure and the size of the money supply.

Players select one of three policy emphases on which their performance is judged. Each policy emphasis provides a score representing the difference between positive points for economic activity and negative points for unemployment, inflation and the balance of trade deficit. The three variants place different penalties for incurring each of the three sources of minus points. The choice of inflation emphasis, for example, means that the player should expect to be penalized relatively more heavily for generating inflation.

When using the game the player is not confined to the experience of one particular set of rigid interrelationships between the economic influences involved. Variability is introduced in two ways. First, there is a random element incorporated in the current account balance between exports and imports. Second, the user is able to change certain key variables such as the marginal propensity to consume, before commencing play, hence altering the way in which the model behaves. This flexibility is introduced in order to explore the implications of different underlying economic relationships and to prevent reduction of the game's educational value through repetition and over-familiarity.

The game may be played by individuals or up to ten teams. Teams do not have to play sequentially: the input of their identification number automatically recalls the requisite information from the disk to allow them to continue where they left off.

Glossary

The following definitions are included to aid the understanding of the reader. The majority of the terms given are fully explained in the main text but are repeated here for ease of reference.

Accelerator principle or theory This relates the level of *investment* to changes in the level of *national income* or *aggregate demand*. It is so called because the coefficient of acceleration is expected to be greater than 1. A change in national income produces a greater or accelerated change in investment.

Aggregate demand The sum total of all the goods and services demanded in the economy over a given period of time.

Aggregate demand management The manipulation of *aggregate demand* by government in an attempt to bring about a desired state of affairs in the economy, e.g., to reduce unemployment.

Capital stock The total value of the stock of plant and machinery capable of producing output accumulated in the economy at any given time.

Classical (school) The term *classical* refers to a school of thought originated by Adam Smith in 1776. The main proposal of the classical economist's was that the economy is inherently self-stabilizing at a full-employment level. This stabilizing influence comes about by way of the market or *price-mechanism*. The free movement of market prices will ensure an efficient allocation of resources to the benefit of the whole society.

Demand curve A mathematical or graphical construct which describes the quantity of a good or service a consumer wishes to purchase at any given price. The demand curve of all consumers may be aggregated to produce the market demand curve for that particular good or service. The sum of the demand for all goods and services at a given price to the aggregate demand curve.

Equilibrium A state in which opposing forces are just balanced. A *market* is in equilibrium when the quantity supplied by producers is just equal to the quantity demanded by consumers (see *Demand curve*; *Supply curve*).

Excess demand The amount by which, given a market price, demand exceeds supply. In *equilibrium* excess demand must be equal to zero (see *Excess supply*).

Excess supply The amount by which, given a market price, supply exceeds demand. In *equilibrium* excess supply must be equal to zero (see *Excess demand*).

Exchange rate The value of a country's domestic currency in terms of the amount of another country's currency that it can purchase, e.g., £1 = $1.50. Each pound will purchase 1.5 American dollars. Flexible or floating rates occur when the value of the exchange rate is determined by supply and demand (see *Demand curve*; *Equilibrium*; *Supply curve*). A fixed exchange rate is one set by the domestic government and monetary authorities. Periodic changes in the fixed rate are referred to as revaluations or devaluations depending on the direction of the change.

Exogenous events Those events outside the influence or control of the domestic government, e.g., a world oil crisis.

Expectations Attitudes or states of mind based on relevant past and current information which influence an individual or group of individuals' anticipation of the nature of future events.

Fiscal Referring to policies concerning government expenditure and taxation. Fiscal policies are those which attempt to influence the economy by manipulation of tax rates, etc.

Full employment In the *Classical* sense this occurs when the labour *market* is in *equilibrium*, i.e., the wage rate is such as to equate the supply of and demand for labour. *Keynesian* economics interprets full employment as that level of employment at which the only labour unemployed is fictional or 'between jobs'.

Function A mathematical expression which stipulates a unique mapping or transformation between two or more variables.

Injection Expenditure on domestically produced goods and services which does not arise directly from the purchase of goods and services by households or from the purchase by domestic firms of the labour services supplied by households. Exports or government expenditure are examples of injections.

Investment Expenditure on fixed plant and machinery.

Keynesian Theories or economists supporting the theories relating to the economics of J. M. Keynes. The implementation of these theories comes broadly under the heading of *aggregate demand management*.

Macroeconomics That branch of economics concerned with the behaviour and determination of the main economic aggregates, such as national income, unemployment and inflation.

Market A market exists when the supplier of a good or service is willing and able to exchange, for *money*, that good or service with those who demand it. Thus the market is essentially defined by supply and demand (see *Demand curve*; *Supply curve*; *Equilibrium*). Markets may be either international, national or regional. When there are no restrictions on the behaviour of traders the market is said to be 'free'.

Microeconomics That branch of economics concerned with the economic decision making of the individual consumer or firm.

Model A theoretical construct used by economists which, whilst being a simplification, attempts to encompass the most important feature of the real world. Modelling is the means by which theories are analysed to make predictions and forecasts about the likely outcome of changes in economic policy or key economic variables, e.g., a model of the labour market would be expected to predict the likely effect on wages and employment of an increase in the demand for labour.

Money Any commodity generally accepted as a means of facilitating purchase.

Monetary policy Pertaining to the control of credit and liquidity in the economy. Used by government singly or in conjunction with *fiscal policy* to attempt to bring about a desired state of affairs in the economy.

National income The total value of all goods and services produced in the economy over a given period of time. Commonly referred to as *gross national product*.

National income multiplier The effect on *national income* of a change in the level of some element of *aggregate demand*. It is called the *multiplier* because a 1 per cent increase/decrease in aggregate demand is expected to induce a greater than 1 per cent increase/decrease in national income. Of *Keynesian* origin.

Nominal (value) The current value or price of a good, service or asset. Taking no account of changes in the *price level*.

Opportunity cost The value of a particular course of action or commodity in terms of alternative commodities or opportunities which must be forgone.

Policy instrument An economic control variable or quantity, such as income tax, which the government may influence in order to achieve its economic objective. (See *Aggregate demand management*; *Fiscal policy*; *Monetary policy*)

Policy target That element of the economy at which a particular *policy instrument* is directed, e.g., control of the money supply may be directed at influencing the rate of inflation. The policy target here is the rate of inflation.

Price level The general level of prices in the economy. An aggregate measure of all prices.

Price mechanism The allocation of resources by the free movement of prices. Also known as the *market mechanism* (see *Equilibrium*; *Market*).

Rate of interest The cost of borrowing, or the reward for lending money.

Real Measurement in terms of physical, tangible characteristics. Having allowance for changes in the *price level.*

Trade-off An expression used in economics to describe the achievement of one objective or state of affairs at the expense of another.

Withdrawal Any direct leakage of expenditure from the domestic economy, e.g., saving, taxation, imports (see *Injection*).

Index